NEW SPROUTS

FROM

AN OLD BRANCH

DOUG MCPHILLIPS

Also, by Doug McPhillips:

NOVELS. AND ALBUMS
From Darkness to Light
Awake to My Gutted Dreams
The Sword of Discernment
Santiago Traveller
I Prophet: towards 2030
Masters at my table
The Guru of Jerusalem
We Are Me Upside Down (Auto-biography)
The Wicklow Way
The Adventures of Ace McDice,
 Stretch Deed & Moonshine Melody
Instant Karma & Grace
The Credo
Reflections of an Old Man
A Writer on the Rock s
Reincarnation of the Assassin
Master of the Arts
The Songs, not the Singer
To Whom It May Concern
Masters of Introspection
The Rise and Rise of a 4th Reich
A Camino Guide Book
Country Camino (Album)
Santiago Traveller (Album)
Soul Fact.(Album

Doug McPhillips April 2024 ISBN.978-1-7636983-2-1

Contents

In life, as in working timber, if we run contra to the grain, we will likely not find bliss but get blisters. It is with the reflection of my former life I, more often than not, went against the grain; I sought the flower only to be ultimately touched by the thorn. Such experiences teach one to hasten slowly and take time out to contemplate the consequences of one's actions before venturing forth, thus making one wiser for the experience.

Words of warning and sound counsel from the author.

CHAPTER 1.

WAITING

Here, I am doing my best to be patient while waiting for inspiration. No, it is not that I am not inspired to write something. I have many ideas floating around in my head and could pluck any one of them out of the pond of the creative well from the muses and begin a new novel of the genre presented to me, much like what had transpired in the former 21 books I have already written and published. No, this time, it is different, for I have reached that stage in the life of another milestone, and it is a release from a former life of which I have drawn much in my worldly expressions to now venture into deeper contemplation. What has drawn me to this is that I graduated to the sensory status of an octogenarian. It is a new and different milestone, an awakening of a different kind. In my former life, I faced many setbacks, disappointments, tragedy, and unbearable suffering, but equally happiness and moments of unexplainable joy and visions of a future that has evolved into reality one way and another.

For the saying here, You, the reader, may examine the term of my natural life into three periods. The first three decades of my single days, the majority of which was tripping the light fantastic in a never-ending stream of pursuits of pleasure and endless dreams of fulfilling my idea of what life was about. For I had achieved little but material rewards and struggled with the constant thought of being on the wrong path from the word go. The second three decades were the time of family responsibilities, pursuing career goals and taking on the burden of debt of creating a home, family, education of children and the ever-increasing turmoil of being on a spinning wheel and running to a standstill. This, like my former single days, went pear shape and ended abruptly with a marriage breakdown and the scattering of my offspring far and wide. The final third of my life has been different, as I struggled to pick up the pieces, giving away the former debauched living of my prior single years and entering a period of adventure and creative pursuits. It has resulted in writing stories about my adventures and subject matters of material and spiritual nature.

Through it all, I worked to improve matters for my bent on reaching my highest potential for the greater good. It has taken until now, in the late evening of my life, to realise that it is essential to learn to wait. The words 'At midnight noon is born' advise that we cannot preempt a new dawn but wait patiently for something new, perhaps bringing a different way of insight to reveal itself. For I am but days into being an octogenarian, so I can't just speak here of milestones achieved but choose to speculate on what may benefit you and what reminds me of time ahead for these latter days that you, the reader, and I may gain some benefit.

In the past, I have been one of the many who live in disorientation from nature and my fellows. However, I have learnt to accept what Robert Frost described as 'taking time out for re-assembly'.

"A visit to the country can often nourish the spirit, for nature is deeply healing. I have long ago realised, but only as an intermediary, that practising taking long walks and eating is beneficial. It has helped in the past to note whatever significant dreams occur during such a period of retreat (making sure to write them down at once before they vanish.) I am more mindful now that we must not try to solve the dreams like crossword puzzles but take them with us for long walks and reflect on what each is trying to tell, for such significant dreams come from an intense part within us where all wisdom is stored. Such times of withdrawal can be crucially important."

We may be near or far from our fellowman, but it is essential to be in that state of contemplation with an eye on the sacred as much as on the breath of nature within. As Khalil Gibran wrote in The Prophet: "Let there be spaces in your togetherness and let the winds of the heavens dance between you. Love one another but make not a bond of love: Let it rather be a moving sea between the shores of your souls. Fill each other's cups, but do not drink from one cup. Give one another your bread, but eat not from the same loaf. Sing and dance together and be joyous, but let each of you be alone. Even as the strings of a lute are alone, they quiver with the same music. Give your hearts, but not into each other's keeping. For only the hand of Life can contain your hearts. And stand together, yet not too near together: For the pillars of the temple stand apart, And the oak tree and the cypress grow not in each other's shadow."

I had come to believe long ago that we of undisciplined nature and uncontrolled passions do not fit the ways of the material world. We are squared pegs that have tried for so long to fit into round holes. We belong to that 1%-3% of the population that is uniquely different. Our path is spiritual rather than material, and it comes as a shock when we realise we have no choice but to accept our uniqueness. We are powerless over what has always been our destiny. Therefore, we can no longer conform to the pattern of this world but be transformed by renewing our minds. Then, we can test and approve God's good, pleasing and perfect will.

So, I recall works previously written, but I had yet to practise— those gems of wisdom in living life on life's terms over a long lifetime. In moments of former contemplation, I had written of lessons learnt to pass on to the reader in acceptance of the consequence of my lot in life in the twilight years of existence. I recalled the lessons of life I learned the hard way, the wisdom and advice from wiser heads that I had not heeded at the time but had to learn before accepting the consequences of my actions. I had reflected on visions of a life as an aftermath of prior wrongful living according to the world's ways and not my heart-soul journey. It is only through this reflection now that I have realised my lot in life and what to pass on to those willing to gain the wisdom that I am still learning for my soul self and you, the reader, mutual well-being.

Much of what has been beneficial to me has come through meditation. 'A journey of a thousand miles begins with a single step.' In other words, one makes a path by walking! So, it is with the practice of meditation. We begin simply by sitting still, being totally aware and listening inwardly—day after day. As Jesus said, 'No one having put their hand to the plough and looking back is worthy of the kingdom of heaven,' we need to remember that when Jesus speaks of heaven, he is not speaking of somewhere hereafter but that the 'kingdom of heaven within you'.

In my former life, I found little time for meditation and prayer. I was far too busy making a living, enjoying the pleasures of life that presented themselves and seeking out what the world had to offer in preference to what the inner world presented to me. It changed when the God of my later understanding turned my life on its head. I suffered much grief and a mental breakdown. It was then that I learnt to meditate, to take on board what nature offers in a spirit of adventure, and it was when I gave up drugs of choice to get through the day. That was a process over the first decade of this latter third of my life. The second decade of this period has been in the primary creative pursuits, which have me now in this time of contemplation and consideration of what is essential to my well-being.

In time, I came to believe that God led me to practice meditation and the repetition of a mantra. It is a single word or a phrase repeated at intervals throughout the day, whether I am cleaning my teeth, sitting on the toilet, preparing a meal, or waiting in a queue. The repetition acts like a monastery bell summoning me to the silence within. The mantra also works in another way when we are in an emotional upheaval or experiencing a setback or challenge; it acts like yeast on the whole of our being, both psychologically and spiritually.

As a recovering alcoholic of some 18 years in the programme of Alcoholics Anonymous, I had forgotten over time how important a mantra is, particularly in the early stages of the recovery process. Early in the process, I used to say the serenity prayer over and over again to starve of mental turmoil and the longing for a drink. " God, Grant me Serenity to accept the things I cannot change, courage to change the things I can, and the wisdom to know the difference." It has been a prayer mantra for Alcoholism since the days of the Fellowship Foundation back in the 1930s.

To consider the process of contemplation and how it applies to our lives, I must return to others and their experiences. Back in 1961, Carl Milton wrote " New Seeds of Contemplation." It sums up what I think I am eluding to in the trim work unfolding here. " *Contemplation is the highest expression of man's intellectual and spiritual life. It is that life itself, fully awake, fully active, fully aware that it is alive. It is a spiritual wonder. It is spontaneous awe at the sacredness of life, of being. It is gratitude for life, awareness, and being. It is a vivid realisation that life and being in us proceed from an invisible, transcendent and infinitely abundant Source. Contemplation is, above all, awareness of the reality of that Source.*

Life can be more than just working for the man. It can be about forging meaningful connections and leaving an impactful legacy. It starts with self-discovery and realising that our passions and dreams can guide our lives.

It seems imperative now that I continue to ask myself, "Why do I do what I do?" I seek answers that resonate with my heart and mind and embrace a way of life rich with purpose and value. The journey may be uncertain, but we can all rediscover the power to shape our paths by pursuing these fundamental questions.

Contemplation is God's way of allowing us to see what we could not see before. It is about nature, people, and you and me. More important than all this is the connection with the God of our understanding, how we act upon the insights we experience through Him, and our human existence with others daily.

In the Gospels, we hear about Jesus and his disciples retreating occasionally to pray. Their ministry didn't allow much time for this, but if they hadn't stopped occasionally, they might have become mindless in their activity. The first step in contemplative action is to stop and reflect. Stopping allows you to pause and acknowledge what you've been doing in your work or personal life. It offers needed rest and helps you move into the next stage of reflection.

"The apostles gathered around Jesus and reported to him all they had done and taught." (Mark 6:30). Jesus and the apostles spoke to each other about all they did, prayed and pondered, and examined their feelings and experiences. Reflecting on our daily and significant experiences helps us discover their deeper meaning.

Reflection may be alone, using prayer or as a group to share intentional faith. What may I learn from these experiences? What might God be telling me through them?

Next, the disciples returned to their busy work, as we must do. The key here is letting your reflection and prayer time inform how you approach your work when you return. You may discover the need for more rest time or that you need to focus more on a particular relationship. Or maybe you find that the activity you've been up to has become dissatisfying. Or perhaps you discover a desire to reinvigorate your job.

Contemplation allows us to renew our active lives (work, play, relationships) so that all we do does not become mindless action but rather glorifies our spiritual connection with the God of our understanding. Then, the cycle repeats. Your activity leads you again into a time of stopping, resting, reflecting, and then returning to activity with greater zeal and purpose. Being contemplative in action means that your active life feeds your contemplative life, which informs your active life. That is what contemplation in action means, and the cycle never ends.

It is at odds with our sense of being in the early stages of contemplation, for it causes us to wonder if we are really receiving God's message or just a distraction of our own making. It is here we need the guidance of masters of the spiritual life. John of the Cross wrote for contemplatives that he wanted to take by the hand, for most are baffled when they reach the crossroads of sudden insurmountable obstacles. On the other hand, when we get to the Way of impenetrable darkness, we must be brave enough to enter through it. We have two roads in answer to our dilemma: meditation and contemplation.

CHAPTER 2.

QUO VADIS

According to a legend first found in the Acts of St. Peter, he met Jesus on the Way when fleeing from Rome. Peter said, 'Domine quo vadis? ('Lord, where are you going? ') Christ replied, 'I am going to Rome to relive my crucifixion again.' Peter went back to Rome, where he gave himself up to be crucified, too.

There are many impurities in our desires, and until they are purified, they are distractions and obstacles to communion with God, to which grace draws us. Impure desires weary, disturb, darken and defile us 'like the tossing sea that cannot keep still; its waters toss up mire and mud, and there is no peace.   (Isaiah 57:20-21)

Where goest thou? The pathway to spiritual awakening is a challenging field to plough. As a confessed alcoholic, I find the steps of AA are the guiding field of experience towards that final awakening, but there is a price to pay. It may take more darkness, pain, and suffering, even in sobriety, before the soil of one soul is ready to plant God's love and direction on our happy road to destiny.

I had once again adopted the habit of daily reflections within the bounds of the AA guidance. However, I still felt not entirely released from my former attachments to material desires and the need for applause. It was true I had not been far forward from death in my pity and suffering self and those suicidal thoughts that once plagued me. My fear in that regard had me on a course of leaving something of value behind. Initially, it was in writing my first book of poems, a novel and an album of songs. I wanted to leave behind more than just a headstone for future generations, but I soon came to believe this was folly and another ecocentric ego notion of life's purpose. God had granted me the will to see through this as I slowly awakened to a new dawning. I had been down the well and into the dragon's mouth, and what emerged was a lotus flower of creative ideas. The old psychiatrist patient in the hospital bed beside me had warned: "In your creative pursuits, be careful of residual parachutes."

The Camino de Santiago seemed a natural path for me to take in search of a transformative state of being in tune with my inner soul. After my first Camino, which pilgrims commonly know as The Way, I summarised what it was for me as an introduction to my website, caminoway.com.au.

"The Way is for the most adventurous and curious of free-spirited travellers. I passed through uninhabited wilderness and traversed towns, villages and urban cities. The Camino was more than just a walk in the woods for me. It inspired a novel, a book of prose and an album of songs that might not have happened had I not taken the journey. I have completed another novel and a new album of songs inspired by two more Camino journeys."

For the next seven years of sobriety, I wrote 20 books in various genres and recorded two more albums of my songs. Despite applause, some financial success, and a sense of satisfaction that somebody could reap divine spiritual good from my creations, it now seems like I had used these creative efforts like a residual parachute in fear of completely letting go in doing God's will.

I had no other answer now but to reflect on the path that led me to creative pursuits to make sense of it all. I still needed a reason to get on with my day, and I felt incomplete unless I was writing or doing something creative that I considered valuable to myself or others. So, my thoughts returned to my mental recovery before my last Camino. It was there that I found a way forward to spend the following years on a personal adventure of mental stability, free of alcoholic behaviour and mind-altering prescription medicines. I had been driven back there for the third time in utter physical exhaustion, mental degradation and spiritual ineptness. My ego still controlled my progress on the spiritual path, not the heart-spirit love I unknowingly sought.

So, it seems fitting to recall my progress through rehabilitation to spiritual enlightenment for you, the reader. The path is narrow and often dark, rough and full of crooked byways, and not well-travelled, so we must endeavour to tread it before we eventually find the right way.

Early in my recovery, I attended counselling sessions with Professor Parker of the " Black Dog" institute. The term "Black Dog" was coined by Winston Churchill during his dark days of depressive mood episodes during WW11 as PM of England. Professor Parker had concluded that I was suffering from the many tragic events that had surrounded my life in the previous year and were the prime cause of my illness. He prescribed a sedative to help me sleep, and I now conclude in hindsight that had I continued along that path of treatment, my depressive state of mind after much rest and recovery would have ultimately left me earlier than it did.

I regularly engage in many types of mediation sessions. Visualise the chakra centres of spiritual power as a spinning wheel, a lotus flower, a bright light, or anything else that works for you—moving from the bottom of your spine upwards to the top of your head. Picturing the chakra in its designated colour, repeat an associated mantra out loud or in your mind. I followed that by just sitting in a quiet space and repeating a mantra. Later, I gravitated to walking on soft grass or sand and feeling the early beneath my feet as I walked, focused heel to toe with each step. I tried various other methods, such as giving devotion to the God of the East, West, North, and South as an animal, reptile, fish, or symbol. Also, in group sessions, we worshipped the sun and the moon, the earth and the ocean's depth in our meditative states. Through it all, I ultimately concluded that deep breathing and focusing on the breath was the best recipe for my recovery.

During early recovery, I retreated to the Mid-North Coast to help heal my mental state and find some peace of mind. I found a small place to live near the beach. My daily routine was to jump out of bed and make my way to the bathroom to do my ablutions, followed by a quick change into a T-shirt, shorts, and sneakers, then make my way to the beach to watch the sun come up, walk for three kilometres along the shore and return to my humble abode to meditate for a half an hour, eat a light breakfast, then pack a knapsack with a can of baked beans, a spoon, piece of fruit and some mixed nuts and adequate water to see me through the day. Afterwards, I would set off on a coastal walk in the bush or find a mountain track to follow in my pensive mood. I would return at night to my sleeping quarters to cook a meal, write poetry, take my sedatives to get some shut-eye and repeat the process the next day. After six months of this way of life, I considered myself well enough to return to the world of materialism and a sense of wellness. I had yet to learn that my future was of living in the world but not being of the world.

So it was only a short time before I was headlong into work, writing books and renovating properties to make ends meet. In the meantime, I attended further meditation sessions, camping out with groups for weekend contemplation and coming to terms with my feelings of being alone with myself, for a God of my understanding seemed not to exist in those times of significant doubt and despair. I had to console myself in the feelings of nature, content to listen to the sounds of silence in the bush or flowing waters in a steam. Even though I felt this nature in a national park amid the city, it was a healing step away from the ever-increasing pace of city life. It was only a short time before I found no alternative but to turn to further help from the medical profession.

My daily routine in my first rehabilitation consisted of a duty to attend meetings for the day's plan and an agenda of daily job breakdown set for all patients. Mine was to lay out the yoga mats first thing in the morning and write up my daily journal, then breakfast and a series of group counselling sessions throughout the day. I was not capable of much more than that and gained little from the first few weeks other than slowly regaining my mental and physical strength. The last week was the most beneficial. A series of what the hospital councillors called 'empty chair therapy." It was simply being in a group and sitting opposite an empty chair. As a participant, we sit imaginatively placing someone in that chair who had psychologically injured us or was instrumental in the suffering of another. We learnt how to apply 'boundaries' and return the shame to the offending party in that chair. It was for me the most rewarding, for I found reconciliation with my long-deceased mother in her childhood abandonment of me and an initial reconciliation with a relative whom I had lost contact with and who had been abused as a child by a so-called religious teacher and a man of faith.

Old habits die hard, is an expression I recall from some guiding spirit of my youth. So, I returned to AA with renewed vigour, determined to find a new pathway to the spirit for my life. Whilst I had set out on many treks in New Zealand in my sobriety, the Camino drew me back to writing the many books and songs that emerged from the muses of my creative spirit. It seemed that whilst I achieved a release from pain and suffering in my long excursions of The Way, I fell into toxic relationships that caused me to come undone more than once in the decade that followed.

The relationship I got involved in on my second Camino in Portugal was toxic from the beginning. It lasted three months in all, and ultimately, I had no option but to return to rehab for the very last time. I had hit a brick wall once again and was in a terrible state of depression, despair of my position and need of great rest to recover from my self-inflicted wounds. It took weeks of rest before I came out the other side and returned to some semblance of normality.

I had been down the medication path for a long time, and it didn't seem to balance the serotonin in my brain to bring peace and some semblance of being a 'Happy Chappy.' So, I volunteered for shock ECT treatment. Electroconvulsive therapy (ECT) is a procedure done under general anaesthesia. During this procedure, small electric currents pass through the brain, intentionally causing a brief seizure. ECT changes brain chemistry, and these changes can quickly improve symptoms of certain mental health conditions. ECT's most common side effects on the day of treatment include nausea, headache, fatigue, confusion, and slight memory loss, which may last minutes or hours. At least, that is what the pamphlet said before my first treatment. I must admit I never suffered many of the effects that my fellow patients had in having the treatment. Apart from fatigue and the loss of consciousness whilst being treated, no more than one might experience any other anaesthetic procedure in a hospital.

After days of ECT treatments, I slowly came out of depression. With the insistent persuasion of the resident psychiatrist, I agreed to take a cocktail of anti-depressant drugs to keep me calm and help in the balance of serotonin in the brain. It seems if I was to be allowed to leave rehabilitation after my days of treatment. I could not be released without the psychiatrist ticking the box, even though I had entered of my own free will. I had argued many times about the treatment of depression with medically prescribed drugs. To my mind, the pharmaceutical companies had the medical profession in the palm of their hands as a pill for every person's cure for mental illnesses. There is documented proof that the industry makes some two trillion dollars a year from prescribed medication, of which there are many kick-backs to the medical profession along the way. I hasten to add that there are mental conditions that some people suffer that, to date, can only be treated by prescribed medication. It also may be noted that ECT treatment does not work for everyone. I consider myself one of the lucky ones who found after many treatments that this methodology of brain wave alterations proved effective in my ultimate recovery.

Still, I had no choice but to agree to the pill-popping treatment for the future as they had already recorded my medical history that I suffered from a depressive illness. To my mind, I did not fit the box that they had me fit into to justify their treatment, and having suffered the massive loss of family, business and friends in a concise space of time; I had concluded that this was the prime cause of my depression and of course my prior habit of attempting to drink my pain away.

I went along with the psychoanalytic pill-popping treatment for the next year and, from time to time, attempted to go off the drugs only to find I was hooked and suffered great pain, nausea and sleepless nights as a consequence. Soon enough, I resigned myself to my condition. By the end of the year, I had begun to make plans for another Camino. So it was that whilst I fumbled my way through a daily ritual of medication to stay level-headed whilst I went about my work a day world and managed to keep a certain amount of peace at night, I was not content to remain that way. Thus, I began planning my next Camino at the end of the year after rehabilitation. I had a plan of what to pack and what my medical needs were whilst on the pilgrimage. I had worked on it for a month or two before venturing to start my journey. In the process, just days before catching a plane destined for Paris, I had forgotten to take my medications. I soon realised that I was feeling much better and resolved to cease medications altogether. Well into the second leg of the flight, the withdrawal symptoms kicked in. Thus, I set out for Spain on the second leg of the flight and began to get violently ill with continuous vomiting, dizziness and unsteady feelings when I walked.

Overnight in Paris before catching the train to St. Jean Pied de Port at the foothills of the Pyrenees mountains, I had concluded that I would continue to go cold turkey off the medication. I would not recommend this to anyone, by the way, as it is a hell of a ride to come off the meds without supervision. Nevertheless, I preserved and walked the drugs out of my system over the next two weeks. Since then, I have had no cause to return to taking any medication, and with the grace of God, the guiding influence of my AA fellowship in staying sober a day at a time through living the steps of the programme, I have not had a repeat of any episodes of depression since.

Pursuing creative activity, writing books, recording songs and constant contact with those in the AA programme who need my assistance has been the healing balm to my daily existence ever since my last major trek some seven years ago. I am not advocating that this is the best cause for anyone else. Still, much of human illness is self-inflicted or not coming to terms with one action or acceptance of circumstances that surround us is a matter of human conditioning in the main; we suffer from a spiritual malady more than a mental or physical one. It is more a matter of learning to observe where we are and, despite any circumstance, to learn detachment from all in the spirit of observation and contemplation without adding attachment. It is to observe the matter or circumstance happening around us and not to be influenced by it. In such a state of peace and acceptance, we may learn great spiritual lessons, influence our bodies and minds to be disciplined, and find a natural spiritual contentment with the God of our understanding.

While the meditative state was once a daily habit for me for a decade, I had long since drifted away from the practice. Only now am I more than ever mindful of its benefits. It is as beneficial as an afternoon nap to refresh my body, rest my mind and calm my spirit.

Therefore, in writing these lines, I am considering the practice again: simply sitting in a comfortable position and scanning my body from head to toe, beginning with one side and continuing down the other. Then, I can breathe deeply from the core of the diaphragm, bringing the whole body into a state of total relaxation.

The diaphragm is the most efficient breathing muscle. It's a large, dome-shaped muscle at the base of our lungs. Our abdominal muscles help move the diaphragm and give more power to empty the lungs. Diaphragmatic breathing helps us use the diaphragm correctly to strengthen it and decrease the work of breathing by slowing our breathing rate, thus reducing oxygen demand with less effort and energy to breathe. During diaphragmatic breathing, we consciously use our diaphragm to take deep breaths. When we breathe normally, we don't use our lungs to their total capacity. Diaphragmatic breathing allows us to use our lungs at 100% capacity to increase lung efficiency.

My former practice taught me that diaphragmatic breathing offers several benefits to the body, including helping to relax, improving muscle function during exercises, and preventing strain. It also increases the amount of oxygen in my blood, making it easier for my body to release gas waste from my lungs, reducing my blood pressure and heart rate.

 I was once a heavy smoker and thought that smoking relieved my stress. All it did was raise my blood pressure when I drew in the smoke, and it gave me a feeling of relief when I exhaled. What followed was long periods of bronchitis brought on by my toxic habit. Again, with God's grace, I gave up the habit of going cold turkey off smoking some five decades ago, just as I had done in giving up prescription medications.

As I write, I am reflecting and must carefully consider my purpose. I want to give myself more reflection, contemplation, and meditative peace. So, I will take time out now to rest from my efforts, guided by the work of great masters of the past who seemed to spend as much time pursuing their creative efforts as they did contemplating, praying, and sleeping.

At the beginning of the next chapter, I am reminded of the Sistine Chapel, a papal chapel in the Vatican Palace erected in 1473–81 by the architect Giovanni dei Dolci for Pope Sixtus1V (hence its name). Although it had many frescoes on its walls by many artists, it is most famous for Michelangelo's Renaissance frescoes on the ceiling, western walls, and the altar. The works depict the Old Testament and the Last Judgment. Michelangelo was paid on a commission basis as ordered by Pope Julius in 1508. It took two years of hard work for the artist to finish the job, often interrupted by the Pope's insistence on Michelangelo to wake up from his slumber and to work. Little did the Pope know that the creative imagination needs as much rest as it does action. So, considering the great minds of the Renaissance period and the genius of modern-day achievements, I devote the next chapter to them.

CHAPTER 3.

ON REST, ART & SUFFERING

The history of great artists and writers records that sleep deprivation was not uncommon. Michelangelo slept for no more than two hours a night but catnapped for short spells up to 20 times a day, mainly while painting the Sistine Chapel. While napping stations are all the rage in trendy millennial workspaces, mid-day sleeps are not new. It was common for people in the pre-industrial age to break up their night's sleep into segments: "first sleep" and "second sleep." But, as legend has it, some of history's greatest thinkers took that further.

Allegedly, Leonardo da Vinci and Nikola Tesla stuck to an almost impossibly strenuous sleep cycle. While the pre-Industrial segmented sleepers had a biphasic routine (hitting the pillow twice a day), da Vinci and Tesla practised the most intense example of polyphasic sleeping (bedtime more than three times a day). One of de Vinci's secrets, or so it has been claimed, was a unique sleep formula: he would sleep 15 minutes out of every four hours for a daily total of only 1.5 hours. Therefore, it appears he was able to gain an extra six productive hours a day. By following this unique regimen, he 'gained' an additional 20 years of productivity during his 67 years." On the other hand, Tesla never slept more than 2 hours per day and walked some 16 kilometres daily, perhaps napping as his way of overcoming sleep deprivation and gaining further creative inspiration. He claimed his father and grandfather did likewise and lived to over 100 years of age.

It is medically well-known that sleep deprivation makes you eat more than you need, drive like a drunken fool, kill your ability to learn, and lack of sleep will eat your brain. While sleep is critical for countless reasons, no one ever said you must soak it all up in one sitting or layer. So, whilst the great masters may well practice a different kind of sleep pattern, my lack of sleep during past works of creative output has done much more harm as I lacked the wisdom of short episodes of shut-eye during the day to make up for the lack of sleep of the previous night.

The habit of long-term work in front of the computer screen to churn out another novel or some follow-up proofreading of work completed would see me write until midnight, sleep for three hours and return to the computer until dawn. Instead of resting in bed, I would get on with the typical day's activity, return to writing in the early afternoon, and repeat the process. I figured that yoga stretches, some sugar-laden sweets or a short walk in the fresh air was enough of a break, but to be sure, I was sleep-deprived for a few years before I changed my habits for the better. I take frequent breaks from the computer these days despite not getting adequate sleep during the night. I rarely return to the laptop after six pm in the evening, and most afternoons, I have a cat nap for at least 20 minutes before getting on with another task. It is paramount that I have a plan of action for the day, but I need to stick to it more religiously. I'm more inclined to do the next right thing for my self-preservation. My routine may include a 30-minute walk after breakfast, phone calls to those of my friends who are suffering some setback in their life and need a friend to download their woes upon or simply chanting away our time together without much thoughtfulness in the conversation. I may then return to contemplation and spiritual thinking before the next task comes to mind, or I refer to a list to see what I have overlooked. Sometimes, ego-centred thinking causes me to lose touch with spiritual connection during my daily activities. A song I recall speaks of life and sums up this journey.

"Leela, Leela, This world is just a game,
Winners lose, and losers win. The game is still the same.
Leela, Leela, this life is just a play,
Those who say don't know, and those who know don't say.
The eyes of the baby behold everything from under,
The eyes of the young man beheld his lady's face with wonder.
The eyes of the older man look upon the flowing river,
What of those whose eyes are one?
They leave this world forever.

And where is the man who can feel it in his heart?
Can he feel it in himself, and then can he reveal it?
Then let him sit and sing and sail the flowing river,
Snakes and arrows cannot go where sound remains forever.

Leela, Leela, this world is just a game,
God will not forget the one who sings his name.
Leela, Leela, this life is just a play,
Those who say don't know, and those who know don't say.

And where is the man who can feel it in his heart?
Can he feel it in himself, and then can he reveal it?
Then let him sit and sing and let his heart grow gladder,
Chant to God until the masquerade no longer matters.

- Lyrics Jody Stecher.

It seems that the two great masters of the Renaissance did not have a kind disposition toward each other's artistic talent. While they may have been born a generation apart, Leonardo Da Vinci could not deny the significance of the young Michelangelo's work. Somebody once told of Leonardo Da Vinci and his friend Giovanni di Gavina passing the public benches at the Palazzo Spini Feroni, near Florence's Church of Santa Trinita, where some men debated a passage in Dante. They called Leonardo, asking him to expound the passage for them. By chance, Michelangelo was passing too, and one of them hailed him. At this, Leonardo declared, "Michelangelo will be able to expound it for you". Michelangelo assumed this was said to entrap him, causing him to reply: "No, you explain – you who have undertaken the design of a horse to cast in bronze but were unable to cast it and were forced to give up in shame." So saying, he turned his back on them and began to depart. Leonardo remained, blushing at these words. Finally, wishing to humiliate his rival further, Michelangelo called again: "And to think those castrated Milanese roosters believed you!"

Michelangelo never wasted time trying to "work on his weakness of 'course manners.' Instead, he focused on his strengths: hard work, ambition, and artistic skills. Eventually, people stopped caring about his "brutish behaviour" and hired him anyway — because of his mad creative talent.

Michelangelo's life is the tale of a disgruntled artist working on a commission he never wanted for four years in uncomfortable and cramped conditions atop a scaffold structure. In his youth,

Michelangelo taunted a fellow student and received a blow on the nose that disfigured him for life. Over the years, he suffered increasing infirmities from the rigours of his work; in one of his poems, he documented the tremendous physical strain he endured by painting the Sistine Chapel ceiling.

While Michelangelo was finishing the ceiling of the Sistine Chapel in 1512, he complained of problems with his vision that may have been an eye disease transitory nystagmus caused by prolonged eye strain. Michelangelo likely suffered from high-functioning autism. He overcame physical, artistic and political challenges whilst painting the Sistine Chapel, which included the difficulty of working at great heights in cramped spaces, mastering the fresco techniques and meeting the demanding expectations of Pope Julius under the political pressures of his time. Michelangelo, the renowned painter and sculptor, had arthritis, but his intense work likely helped him keep using his hands until he died. The constant chiselling, hammering and painting accelerated his joint pain.

Leonardo da Vinci faced many challenges during his life. For instance, he came from a broken home with more immediate challenges. He was born an illegitimate child. However, he also had those more significant (more abstract) challenges placed on him by the doctrines of the Church. Leonardo certainly seemed to suffer from the symptoms of adult ADHD, including constant procrastination, the inability to follow through or complete tasks and being easily distracted. He was in constant physical pain and ultimately could not hold a palette or brush but managed to complete his masterpiece "Mona Lisa" in the early 1500s, and from 1513 to 1516, he worked in Rome, maintaining a workshop and undertaking various projects for the Pope.

He continued his studies of human anatomy and physiology, but the Pope forbade him from dissecting cadavers, limiting his progress. Whilst he was never satisfied in his creative pursuits, he enjoyed the ride to the fullest. Reportedly, his last words were: " I have offended God and mankind because my work did not reach the quality that it should have."

Fast forward to the 20th century and the brilliant but tortured world of Nikola Tesla. Imagine being stricken with blinding flashes of light that envelop your mind and fill your brain, but in those blinding flashes is contained a vision that solves a problem that has been racking your brain or the idea for an invention. Nikola Tesla, best known for his work on alternating-current electricity, was inspired by this. He gained inspiration from those visions, which propelled him to be a prolific inventor. Like many great minds in scientific history, he had a somewhat tortured life.

Tesla read voraciously and had an eidetic memory, going beyond the visual recall of a photographic memory. He is said to have envisioned complete diagrams of inventions, sometimes working only from memory, not bothering to draw them. He spoke seven languages. Like many great scientific minds, as I have previously stated, he required little sleep and was reported once to have worked 84 hours straight without stopping to eat or rest. It may well be true that eccentricity often comes with brilliance. Tesla had obsessive-compulsive disorder, which compelled him to do things in threes, including only inhabiting a hotel room that was divisible by the number three. He had an obsession with pigeons and an aversion to women wearing earrings, contributing to his reputation as eccentric. Tesla suffered a nervous breakdown when as a young man and may have had dementia before his death. He never married.

Did Tesla believe in God or science? **He says**, "In my heart, I am deeply religious, though not in the orthodox sense of that word. Our greatest secrets remain but have not yet awakened to us. "His autobiography states, "The gift of mental power comes. From God, a Divine Being, and if we concentrate on that truth, we become in tune with this great power. My Mother had taught me to seek all truth in the Bible; therefore, I devoted the next few months to studying this work."

As mentioned, he spoke several languages and invented the radio, remote control, and alternating current. He was also a complex human being. Most of the quirky things said about him are perhaps because he suffered from OCD. For example, he would walk around a block three times before entering a building, requiring his cup to have ice cubes in multiples of three, etcetera.

After his death at the age of 86, alone in the New York hotel room he called his home, much of his work was put away for future consideration by the U.S. government and declared "top secret," in part because for years Tesla had worked on a "death ray" that was to be a "super weapon" to end all wars. Most of his inventions are still in use today, as are the designs of his weapons, which a military power may use in future wars.

undoubtedly, one may suffer much for art's sake or be inspired to creative output due to suffering. My life experiences, as an outcome of suffering much tragedy in my life some two decades ago, I fell into the depth of depression and extreme anxiety. When I emerged from the dragon's mouth of the night of the soul, I was awakened to a lotus flower of creative ideas. Over the past decades since my recovery, I've written 20 books on various genres and written and recorded three albums of my songs, before which I had no idea this talent lay dormant within me.

It is worthy to note the words of writer Stephen deLay in his thesis on Suffering and Salvation: A Note on Art: [Regardless of what has been told of suffering, the reply we muster in response only glances off the surface of what our words struggle to retrieve from the abyss of pathos, having hoped to install a castle of significance upon the tidal shores of intelligibility. The effort is in vain. Our utterance, as the sandcastle, soon disappears. The waves of suffering never decrease, which is why everything, including the words themselves responsible for expressing the grief that has ejected them, eventually is sucked out back to the unbounded sea of silence to rejoin the whirlpool of experience within whose muteness from whence they had so fleetingly just bubbled forth. And so, as suffering by the very essence of its amplitude perpetually defies our capacity to speak adequately in the wake of what its passage has given us to understand, the following remarks, which will attempt to say something on the matter nevertheless, are brief. And a not-unfitting choice! In the end, a note on suffering does as well as the treatise.]

[Art is not salvation. That is the central thought. As apparent as the lesson may seem, to exalt art in this way is to bow before the postmodern commonplace, one so prevalent today that we hardly notice it, that sees suffering as a passage to nothing beyond itself. Most think that we suffer without end or, more fundamentally, without purpose. And if art comes to be treated as a form of salvation, as our postmodern condition does, it is because art grapples with the pangs of suffering. And when attention turns to suffering, the issue of salvation cannot be far off. Why does art fail to save us from the trials of suffering? We are powerless to make sense of it. We are powerless to make sense of our powerlessness to justify suffering. We are helpless in handing over to artificial salvation, and in our delusion, having affirmed the death of God, find that Life accordingly is reduced to an aesthetic phenomenon, and it is far from clear that this is a good thing. Life becomes wholly a matter of style, of deciding how one as an individual will make suffering one's own. Hence, today, the venerable (and sacred!) idea that there is a transcendent meaning to suffering is a notion many have learned to laugh at.]

Frederich Nietzsche, a German classical scholar, philosopher, and critic of culture, became one of the most influential modern thinkers. He observes that our modern form of existence suffers from a crisis of meaning. In the magazine Gay Science, he states that giving one's character Art makes it possible to endure existence but that its distinctive style, one must "turn oneself into a work of art."

Nietzsche views a thinking that remains ambivalent about the value of existence. On the one hand, from the beginning of his 'The Birth of Tragedy ', he desires to reject the pessimistic thesis that man cannot justify life. On the other hand, it isn't easy to see how anybody can affirm existence. For what it is without the intermediary of illusions. Such affirmation will be possible only as an aesthetic phenomenon for life to be a statement of fact. And that, as The Birth of Tragedy states, here means an affirmation entailing illusions will be necessary to tolerate life. Thus, when Nietzsche later in his career, particularly in The Gay Science and elsewhere, stated that art struggles against pessimism, this is a departure from his initial position, which seemed to assert that it is impossible to affirm life if faced with what it is. To say, then, as Nietzsche does in The Will in Power, "There is no such thing as pessimistic art—Art affirms," simply raises the question of what exactly it is affirming. Life is to be sure, but is it seen fully in its truth or illusions in some way or another?

In The Birth of Tragedy, life is not affirmable without recourse to illusion, whether Apollo's beauty, lust, chaos or a combination. As Nietzsche clarifies, art does not provide mind knowledge that justifies life. Instead, it gives us natural solace and placative illusions in the form of myth that make life bearable. An illusion, not the objective truth, makes life worth living.

In this sense, life is worth living as an aesthetic phenomenon only because only art makes what would otherwise be unbearably tolerable. Life is to be endured with the help of illusion, not embraced for what it is. Without the aesthetic illusion of Apollo's beauty, we would lack the strength to accept the ugly truth of what we could not bear.

CHAPTER 4.

A GLIMMER OF HOPE

At the beginning of Fear in Trembling, in the section entitled "Eulogy on Abraham," Kierkegaard describes the view of the world as a cruel and vicious primal oneness to be ignored on the one hand, but on the other as a wild frenzy of chaos to be embraced. If a human being did not have an eternal consciousness, if underlying everything there was only a wild, fermenting power that writhing in dark passions produced, be it significant or insignificant a vast, never. In a meditation named "The Happiness of Eternity," Kierkegaard says that seeing the end of suffering means seeing it in perspective, which means humanity must view it in light of eternal life. Then, its burden is not so heavy as when eternity is rejected. Is it not when the suffering, as the impatient man expresses it, is without meaning or purpose?" Suffering as without a point, he says, is to have discarded eternity. The joy of anticipating eternal happiness makes suffering heavier than it is or needs to be. If human beings did not have an infinite consciousness, if underlying everything there were only a wild, fermenting power that writhing in dark passions produced everything, be it significant or insignificant, if a vast, never appeased emptiness hid beneath everything, what would life be then but despair?

The creative mind emerges from the darkness, and I do not doubt my own experiences that a powerful force more significant than the self is instrumental in this happening. Creativity is, and perhaps will always be, a great mystery. Though academic research explanations may be and measurements will be made, the simple phenomenon of something new coming into being is akin to the miracle of life itself. Some may be content with technical explanations and strictly materialist accounts, but the glimmer of mystery remains for many more.

I had come to a mystical side of myself that could not be expressed in words or through worldly deeds, a cause that could be fulfilled only by the spirit that was central to the candle that burned within - a candle that, to me, was a symbol of life itself, a flame that burned at a deep level, projecting light into the darkness. And in the flickering awareness, I could almost hear a message: "Exist; stay alive; survive". Here, for the first time, I was learning about my true nature, being aware of my body, my mind, and the true spirit within.

I had come from darkness and had tried to clutch too tightly to the past when my worldly claims engulfed me. Yet here I was now, surrendering my all, falling moment by moment into that surrendering and risking falling into the unknown, falling into the fearful dragon's mouth of self-acceptance, with the fear of falling into a pit of darkness where the dragon lived, where there was no light, only darkness, of weeping and gnashing of teeth. In my mind, it would be in the bottomless pit where the dragon lived, to descend into the dragon's mouth, and I would find the dragon's mouth turn into a lotus flower of creative ideas.

There, I had fallen part of the way when I lost everything I thought life was about. Wife, friends, business and wealth had left me, and it was then that I had turned to other lovers; lovers who brought me their pain in my pain, comfort in my agony, illusion in their mystic lover-rites. I'd had a sense of the Goddess for a brief moment, only to find disenchantment and, once more, illusion—a cover of the inner truth I was seeing now for the first time in my life. I had turned to regain the respect of my children only to find that they had moved on, as was their right, and all I could do now was to be there for them in the event of their fall; be there now, in a sober mind.

I had struggled to regain the wealth I once possessed, only to find that pursuing wealth was of little comfort to me apart from the need for food, clothing and shelter. I felt apart from the world I once knew and realised that my heart no longer craved anything that was once my sure-fire way of enthusiasm for living. I had taken an inner truth of honesty to myself, an open-mindedness and a willingness to grow, a willingness not to worry, acceptance, and belief in living with whatever comes my way. I began to relax then, to allow the coil of the wound-up spring within me to unwind slowly, let go and trust in God without definition.

I was coming to a vacuum and was surrendering and letting it sink into the marrow of my bones. I knew it was time again to fall into the pit. On previous falls into the pit, I had taken a parachute of meaningless clutched possessions and wild ego notions, a crutch to lessen the impact of the fall. The residual inner nervous tension had remained, so I was going without a parachute, forethought, or plan this time. I knew that I had to surrender to win, to give way to keep, to surrender to get well, to die to live! So, the new life of the inner spiritual was unfolding. I was learning to let go and allow the inner core of my being to take hold of something from nothingness. It was where I now believed the universe began: that something that was my God.

I discovered within myself a way of cutting through to the reality of everything that comprised my life and an enlightened ability to judge and act with wisdom; I found, symbolically, a Sword of Discernment, a tool to carry as my staff of action, my brand of reason. I had a choice now: to use my Sword of Discernment like a knight of old, to go with the flow, friendly and easy, and accept with free will whatever comes along, to use my inner discernment with wisdom and understanding whenever and wherever I may think fit; to pursue or not to pursue in consideration of who and what I was beginning to realise I was, am and will be; the right to act or not to act according to the dictates of my consciousness, of my heart and the beauty that lived within me. I determined to adopt an accord of consciousness with every human being with whom I would come in contact on my outward and inward journey: a journey of understanding, a journey of nature being both cruel and kind, of being as vigilant as a female serpent within my inner being on the pathways of my life, and as innocent as a dove. A freedom nothing bar death could take from me – my freedom of choice for living.

In the past, I often ran against the grain, resulting in splintered wounds. I am running with the inner river's flow and the current in ocean waters. I knew it was not the old ways of strength, enthusiasm, leadership and dogma that would project me like an arrow towards some designated target; instead, it was to be a slow road, one day at a time, moment to moment, using the coiled spring's thread to unwind, unravel and let go to achieve inner calm. I was learning to use no force and to let go to achieve inner calm. I was learning to let the force within take hold, allowing time to heal and grow; I knew I needed to go with the grain, as an artist working with wood, in time, knows.

I knew within my heart of hearts existed a Sword of Discernment, and I longed for an outward expressive symbol of this inner need and courage. I would let go of my inner turmoil and take a journey of the spirit – my spiritual heart expressed in a tangible symbol. I could think of no better way than the way of St. James, the apostle, whose symbol was a real Sword of Discernment; the sacrificial cross of St. James, the fleury fitch, whose sword blade signifies the sword of a warrior.

I would follow the path of St. James. The Moor-slayer, on The Camino Way, where I would lay down my burdens and walk the traditional Way that so many pilgrims had walked before me. I knew the outward expression I sought would manifest into the sword of St. James. Like the Spanish who fought and conquered the Moors so many centuries ago, their vision of the Saint on a white steed advancing before them holding aloft a fiery red sword of Santiago leading their charge and taking them to victory, I, likewise, would venture forth on the road to Santiago, leading ever onward with a courageous cry, to the quest that pierced my heart.

I would walk The Camino de Santiago! Whilst I would seek a symbolic sword as proof of my journey, I knew that my Sword of Discernment would be more than merely a sword. I knew I would express in words the cry of my heart, the link I had to my past journey. My current turmoil would be in my spiritual quest. I would venture forth with hope and confidence despite the night of the soul. I did not yet know the events that would unfold due to walking my Camino. The thought of a new dawning after the long night gave me the courage to proceed. The night was darkest just before dawn, and I ventured forth despite the sword that pierced my soul.

And so it was that I had tramped The Way of St. James to Santiago, not once but three times over the next decade. It was healing, an in-depth connection to the heart and as much a journey inward as a mental and physical adventure. I learnt a lot about living on the road as a pilgrim. Equally, I knew that chasing an illusion of love leads to more heartache and ruin. Perhaps the most significant insight was the influence of the muses of creativity that not only influenced my writing and songs but haunted me until I committed myself to putting these ideas into action in books and my music outputs.

For a time, I just had to retread the weary way in my thirst for more creative expression. Not only did that prove exhausting, but it ultimately damaged my health, and I needed to take time out for recovery. So it was after repeating the same process I came to accept that one cannot drive creative expression but must wait until I am inspired to complete more calmly and collectively. The discipline of waiting has never come easily for me, and I still suffer from this dilemma to my detriment. I am learning to hasten slowly and trust in the slow work of God as much as the creative output generated from my actions.

The learning curve teaches us about feelings and desires that are part of our nature and that happen without our wanting them. We need not be disturbed, but we should take these as they come with some time to wait and see. Think through the process without disturbing the neutral flow that will go away if it is meant to.

Let us not fall into the trap of not consenting to produce good works, as we may be tempted to produce evils. While making them, we think that the passions and disturbances we produce are defiling and holding us bound; that is not the case.

In the long run, what we produce is all about purifying our distractions, overcoming obstacles to communion with, and embracing the influences of the God of our understanding. Our desires and artistic outpouring may be weary, disturb, and darken us like the tossing sea that cannot stay still without peace. They do afflict us and keep us bound as happened with the masters of old.

So, let us now look at contemplative prayer.

We must learn to wait, sit back and allow peace to bring stillness again. Only by doing this will we have a heart that is not contrite. In offering us the sublime gift of contemplation, God is offering us our most profound spiritual and ultimate desires. What is the use of giving pleasure to our unpurified senses, imagination, and emotions if it ultimately no longer provides pleasure? Our feelings may rebel, but God is granting us an immense favour. God is offering God's self to us. Even in our moments of prayer, we can no longer raise feelings of devotion at will. Thinking about the mysteries of faith sometimes gave us consolation, but now it makes us dry and distracted.

The difficulty we encounter in the early stages of contemplative prayer might cause us to wonder if we are receiving contemplation from God. Could we be caught up in distractions of our own making because of infidelity or carelessness? Are we losing our belief and our fervour? We surely need guidance here, not from the masters of art, science, and the worldly, but from the recognised masters of spiritual life.

The fact is that, ultimately, we cannot purify our senses, feelings, and emotions. Only God's love can do that. So now we must hand everything over to God and focus on responding humbly and faithfully to whatever discipline God is gracing us to undertake. We need to learn to look to God and to wait on God. We can no longer achieve a quiet communion with God as we used to. Is this because God is weaning us off such attractive but not thoroughly purified pleasures? God is drawing us beyond the limits we can attain through our efforts. God wants to take us where our hearts wish to be but where we cannot go while holding on to control.

The lack of feeling in our meditation and prayer can be painful, but we are learning about our limitations. We are learning humility and reliance on God. We are learning to live by faith. Any experience of pleasure is now recognised as a sheer gift of grace. We did not fully understand grace growing up in a Christian religious doctrine. We were taught: "Grace is a supernatural gift imposed on us by God for our salvation." It seemed we were saddled with it whether we liked it or not. It seems now that this 'sheer gift of grace' can be expressed positively or negatively. It functions as sunlight, breeze, and gravity, and it also functions as grace.

Sadhguru, an Indian yoga mystic and author, expresses it this way: "Gravity is trying to pull you down; the breeze is trying to blow you away; the Sun is trying to burn you up; grace is trying to pluck you off the planet. If you want to express the same in positive terminology, the Earth is trying to hug you; the breeze is trying to cool you; the Sun is trying to warm you; grace is trying to make you grow. Grace is trying to pluck you out of the limitations that keep you stuck."

For the most part, it may seem that we will not experience any pleasure and, therefore, any 'sheer gift of grace' for the present. Perhaps it is because something very precious happens in the depths of our being, and God does not want us to be distracted. If you are used to living at this depth, you will miss the more surface feelings, which can be pretty painful.

Depending on how much we need to be purified and how much courage we have to allow this purifying, we may find ourselves in this arid place for a long time. However, we can be sure that God will always graciously offer us the strength to endure. 'No testing has overtaken you, which is uncommon for everyone. God is faithful and will not let you be tested beyond your strength, but the testing will provide the way out so that you may endure.'(1 Corinthians 10:13).

Each person's experience here will be different. Some of us will experience more consolation. It may be because we are already humble, unattached, and readily surrender to love. On the other hand, it may be because we do not dare to go through the purifying fire of love, and God meets us on the surface where we are used to meeting. We forfeit the attraction to the depths that we are afraid to explore.

Suppose we are to enter full communion with God. In that case, we must wean ourselves off surface feelings of consolation, surrender our reason, and live by faith, however painful and bewildering the process may be. We will be encouraged to continue on this path if we recognise that God's love is taking us into our souls' deep and dark recesses, where our senses may feel nothing and our understanding cannot guide us. Since we cannot see God, we must long for God in the darkness.

'This secret, peaceful and loving infusion from God, which is contemplation, liberates the spirit from subjection to the senses, and calms the senses themselves little by little in this night, thus permitting us to have free and peaceful commerce with God, who communicates God's Self to it through the gifts of the Holy Spirit.'Marie-Eugene- I am a daughter of the church.

'Softened and humbled by hardship and other trials, we become meek concerning God, ourselves, and others. Now, we are no longer angry with ourselves and disturbed because of our faults, nor are we with others because of theirs. We are no longer displeased with God because God does not quickly make us holy. These times of dryness, therefore, cause us to journey in all purity in the love of God since we are no longer influenced as previously in our actions by the pleasure and enjoyment of the actions themselves but only by a desire to please God.

John of The Cross. (Night 1.13)

In contemplative prayer, we realise that we are surrendering ourselves to love. Since God is not an object of unmediated human experience, God remains beyond the direct grasp of our human facilities. Contemplative loving, therefore, occurs in the 'darkness' of faith.

When we accept to be guided by faith, we are reunited with God and guided along the way, inspired by God, though our intellect cannot see the path. God is leading us on the way of love. Learning to rely solely on faith can be quite painful as we grieve for the kinds of meditations that we previously had and the pleasure they brought us. However, if we surrender ourselves to God, we will experience an even deeper and richer delight.

Edith Stein, in Ideas from The Science of the Cross, pages 25-28, points out the rich symbolism in John's description of the lack of pleasure in these sense faculties as a 'night'.

On the one hand, night envelops us and all things; it threatens to swallow us up; what it hides is still there but indistinct, invisible, without form; it impedes movement and paralyses our faculties; it indices fear, it condemns us to solitude and is a foretaste of death.

On the other hand, night softens and smooths what hard, sharp, or crude is. It reveals subtle features that are lost in daylight. It drowns out the noises of the day. It quietens the spirit, free from the busyness of the day, and gives deep, gentle repose. So, it is with the mystic night of infused contemplation that arises from within.

In our contemplation, prayer and repose, we seemingly become at one with the Godly forces of nature, which we may perceive as grace. It may come in the force of a feeling of spiritual wholeness with creation, a sense of the presence of something greater than self impeding on our restlessness to bring us calm and well-being. Western Christians understand grace to be a spontaneous gift from God to humanity- " generous, free and unexpected and undeserved"- that takes the form of divine favour, love, compassion, and a share in the holy life of God. In the Eastern Orthodox Church, grace is the uncreated Energy of God.

Actual grace is that special assistance which the Holy Spirit, the third person of the Trinity of Father and Son, grants us to enlighten our minds, inspire and guide our wills to do good works and avoid the evil of our character defects in any particular situation. It consists of temporary gifts of divine light for our minds and divine powers for our hearts.

The problem of resolving fear has two aspects. We shall have to try for all the freedom from fear we can attain. Then, we shall need to find both the courage and the grace to deal constructively with the issues of whatever fears remain.

CHAPTER 5.

GRATITUDE OF GRACE

Many teach grace is getting what we don't deserve, but that is only the 'warm and fuzzy' part of grace. Love is unconditional, but grace always has conditions. Many don't know or don't teach it, resulting in some very off-balance teaching and understanding of the body of Christ. People think grace means freedom, and it does. But the freedom of grace doesn't mean being free to do anything we like, but rather a freedom to serve the Lord. God told Moses to tell Pharaoh, "Let my people go so they may serve me." Not just take them out of slavery to freedom for freedom's sake, but free so they may walk with God. (Exodus 7:16)

Grace always has conditions. You may love your puppy unconditionally, but your grace to them has conditions. At some point, you expect them to stop pooping all over the house, to stop chewing up the pillows, to stop biting the ankles of people who enter your home. Grace expects them to grow up. You may love your child unconditionally but expect certain things from them. Love is unconditional, but grace is not. Grace always has conditions. In every instance of grace seen in scripture, the conditions and limitations of that grace are stated. The foundation of everything relating to salvation is this truth: John 3:16: "For God so loved the world that He gave His only begotten Son, that all who believe in Him will not perish, but have everlasting Life."

"God so loved the world that He gave His only begotten Son"— that is grace. The condition is this: "All who believe in Him will have eternal life." The consequences are clear: God loves you, so He sent Jesus. You won't have God's life if you don't receive grace by believing in Jesus. God's love is unconditional, but the grace of salvation is not. There are conditions attached. Salvation comes through Jesus.

Grace always requires the recipient of grace to handle the grace offered responsibly. There is always accountability within the bounds of grace. If a parent gives the car keys to their 17-year-old, that is grace. Expecting them to be home at 9 pm (21:00) with the car clean and intact is the purpose and limitation of that grace. Cross that line where grace ends, and the 17-year-old will face judgment. No more car for a week, maybe grounded, maybe worse. There are expectations within the grace of salvation to grow up in Christ, to want to walk with Him, to get to know the Father, and to be morally upright. Grace has expectations attached.

Early Christians, who often faced character defects and didn't want to discipline themselves to overcome those ways, started accepting themselves as 'God made me this way', so they felt they could live however they wanted, and God was okay with that.

The core belief (which came from pagan cults) was that matter was evil – the natural world was cruel. And being spiritual was good. So because Christ paid for humanity's deceptive nature, they were in grace and free to live however they wanted, for the natural world, including their earth-bodies, were evil, so passing away. To them, freedom came from 'knowing' their body is evil and their spirit is born again and sound, so they were free to live ungodly lives because they knew 'the Christ' was in everyone deep inside, and the natural world would one day pass. Sound familiar? Gnosticism removes the accountability requirement to our fellow man and God because they 'know better'.

Some then and now explain away verses in the epistles and the words of Jesus that tell us to confess (admit) our sins or 'faults' to God and one another to justify their sinful behaviour. Repentance is one of the foundational principles* in the doctrine of Christ and the first word of salvation. To say otherwise is to turn God's grace into a license for their sin. *Hebrews 6: 1-2; Acts 2: 38, Matthew 18: 15-16, James 5: 16, I John 1: 7-9. The failure to understand grace always has limits and boundaries, which also causes many well-meaning Christians to be taken advantage of. They show grace over and over to family or friends, yet the recipient never uses that grace to change their lives or situation – they keep returning for more. Christians who don't understand grace think God wants them to give and give until they are broke and exhausted. They feel caught between what God wants them to do and their grace-abusing friend or family member.

St. Paul in Romans 7:19-27 wrote:[I don't want to do what is wrong, but I do it anyway. But if I do what I don't like, I am not the one doing wrong; sin living in me does it. I have discovered this principle of life—that when I want to do what is right, I inevitably do what is wrong.] Despite his character defects, Paul's purpose was clear: to spread the good news of the saving Power of God to the Gentiles by embracing the crucified Christ and, by his death and resurrection, be saved. Paul never wavered from his purpose despite opposition, persecution, and imprisonment. He remained steadfast in his mission; Paul stresses that mere knowledge of the Law isn't sufficient for righteousness; obedience is critical. The primary message is that salvation ultimately relies on God's grace and the Gospel of Jesus Christ, knowing that God had called him and would sustain him, as human efforts and consciences alone cannot secure salvation. ROMANS 7:13-25

Jesus never came to bring us peace in an earthly sense; instead, his most controversial recorded text in Biblical history is so often misunderstood. "Think not that I come to bring peace on earth; I came not to bring peace but to bring a sword." The words are one of Jesus' most controversial statements and were never meant to be taken literally. When Peter took a sword and cut off the ear of one of the soldiers who came to take Jesus from the garden of Gethsemane, Jesus, it is written, rebuked him and told him to put away the sword. He had also stated, according to the bible, "He who lives by the sword will die by the sword." Jesus was reportedly The Prince of Peace, yet His words relating to the sword were intended to emphasise its use only figuratively. Jesus' sword of discernment is perhaps more accurate, as He pointed out to His followers that following Him was not easy. It is historically written that His way was not to be the way of the world but a heavenly way of the spirit. He would divide and conquer with discernment, using His inner power and energy for the good of humanity. Without peace, He would divide the people using His Sword of Discernment, dividing son and father, daughter and mother, to achieve His purpose as The Prince of Peace.

Many Christians, even those who help people grow, misunderstand grace. They usually think that grace means forgiveness or the absence of condemnation, and the God of grace is the one who forgives. But while forgiveness expresses God's grace, grace is much bigger than just forgiveness. Theologically, grace is unmerited favour. This definition has two important implications.

1. As I have said, favour means that God is for us and not against us. He is on our side and desires good for us and not evil.

2. His favour cannot be earned; even if it could be, we do not have the means to earn it. We cannot merit it. Therefore, he will freely give us things we cannot provide ourselves.

Practically, these two implications of grace support the entire growth process. To grow, we need things that we do not have and cannot provide, and we need to have a source of those things who look favourably upon us and do things for us for our good. In AA, The Big Book promises the newcomer a new manner of living and a happier relationship with life. The way depends on working the Twelve Steps, which may initially feel intimidating, foreign or uncomfortable. However, the only requirement for AA membership is a desire to stop drinking. If someone shows up, stays sober and tries their best, they are well on their way to fulfilling those Promises.

Steps 8 and 9 of the AA 12-step Recovery Program teach the importance of *making amends* with family, friends, and loved ones. Though grace is given freely, receiving it when we feel undeserving can be challenging. When we feel undeserving of God's grace, there may be a deep-rooted cause stemming from a painful experience in the past.

Of the 12 steps, Step 9 is often considered particularly challenging. I understand why examining Step 9's goals and possible outcomes will be necessary.

But, as difficult as it is, completing this step can provide an immense sense of relief and newfound hope for the future. At the heart of this step is the need for forgiveness and restoration—forgiving yourself, forgiving others, and making amends. The ninth step is essential in the recovery journey. Step 9 stipulates, "Make amends wherever possible except when to do so would injure them or others." Making direct amends requires the individual to correct their mistake. This action can demonstrate the person's new way of life in recovery. It goes beyond simply apologising to taking steps to right a wrong. Whenever possible, those in recovery are encouraged to make direct amends face-to-face with those they'd harmed while living in addiction.

One of the most essential words in Step 9 is "direct." In some programs, you're encouraged to forgive others or work through the guilt and shame you feel towards others alone, without the other party's involvement. Yet, to be truly successful at forgiving and releasing past wrongs, you must go directly to the individual you've hurt. The spiritual transformation will likely occur when you go directly to the person.

You also face the problem head-on. You can't push it to the side or avoid it because of embarrassment. The problem is there, and that person is in front of you. You cannot (and should not) prevent the pain. I also hasten to add the biblical guidance of Matthew 18:22: "Jesus says we should forgive someone seventy times seven in response to a question from Peter about how many times to forgive a brother who sins against him. Peter asks if forgiving seven times is appropriate, and Jesus responds not seven times, but seventy times seven."

Sometimes, we need to metaphorically surround ourselves with God's grace to deal with someone who perceives that we are still guilty of not making amends for past actions even if we believe we have done all we can do. Such a person is still holding on to a grudge and is not satisfied with our apology for past behaviour or seems to be trying to justify old habits of the past. In those instances, if we can come face to face with the offended party, we may have to accept their angry outburst or seemingly jealous fixations as our progression on the spiritual path in recovery, or for that matter, their own. I can only state that trust in God's grace to see you, though in those circumstances, is the best course of action. It is most important to shut up and listen to their gripe. Only then will progress be made, but it may not always be so. Then, all one can do is accept the consequences of that and move on. However, it doesn't mean we should avoid contemplating another approach using the Jesus principle of turning the other cheek seventy-seven.

When you make amends, how you look and feel about situations changes. You can gain clarity about what happened and what should have happened. You also gain some relief from the guilt you feel. Letting go of that guilt can be very healing.

Some of these things can happen to the other person in the process. They may find resolution and understanding about the past. They may discover they can forgive, too. Or, they may gain more significant insights about addiction and commit to being a more supportive person in their recovery. Sometimes, the outcome can be uglier and downright disappointing. The other party may be non-receptive, for example. They may refuse to meet at all or refuse to listen to what you have to say.

Even so, you will have done all you can to take responsibility for the past—and there's a level of peace and freedom in that as well. How the other person responds to our amends is out of our control. At least you have done your best and can now move on. Step 9 is the next in recovery, regardless of how the other person responds. It's not possible to forget what happened. But by facing reality and the long-term impact of your actions and making amends to those you've hurt, you can make peace with the past, put it behind you, and move forward.

God puts us in situations of his guidance at the right time for our welfare, and we learn to grow spiritually by trusting in God's grace. We may contemplate and give over to the spiritual with prayer and meditation, or it may come in listening to spiritual music or reading Psalm 23, "The Lord is my Shepherd," for example.

I must not forget that it was powerless over alcohol that led me to the doors of AA, beaten and having no other cause but to seek help. Here, I was the suggested steps as a program for recovery. I discovered in Step 1 of the AA Steps to Recovery that we were powerless over alcohol and ultimately came to realise that we were also impotent over people, places and things. Soon, I came to Step 2. Here, I 'woke up' to the fact that some power greater than self could restore me to sanity. [Here it was, that I had to learn to trust in a higher power.]

In Step 3, after much contemplation and guidance from fellow AA members in the recovery process, I came to turn my will and life to a God of my understanding. It was then and only then that I began to understand God's healing power through the AA Steps to recovery. In step 4, I was encouraged to make a fearless and moral inventory of myself.

Being still raw to newfound recovery, I sought guidance through The Big Book, the basis of Text for Alcoholics Anonymous and help from another alcoholic whom I selected to guide me in this undertaking. Thus, I came to Step 5: "admitted to God, myself, and another human being the exact nature of my wrongs. Then, I made a list of the persons I harmed and became willing to make amends to them all. So I turned to God to guide me, and in Step 6, I became entirely ready to have God remove all character defects. So, I focused on my comprehension of a higher power and (Step 7) humbly asked Him to remove my shortcomings.

In Step 8, I continued to 'make a list of all the persons I had harmed and became willing to make amends to them all.' Step 9. 'Made direct amends to such persons wherever possible, except when to do so would injure them or others.' As I have previously reiterated, these two steps are still a work in progress for me. I am now more than ever mindful of my many hidden character defects, and it is to this end, I must learn to have more faith and trust in a God of my understanding and the AA programme for guidance. Thus, Step 10, ' continuing to take personal inventory and when we're wrong, prompt admission to it,' is essential in my recovery progress. In previous chapters, I reviewed Step 11.' Through prayer and meditation to improve our conscious contact with God as we understand Him, praying only from the knowledge of his will for us and the power to carry that out.

Step 12 is the most challenging part of recovery because it involves putting the spiritual part of the programme into practice by considering others before myself. " Having had a spiritual awakening as the result of these steps, we tried to carry this message to alcoholics and to practice these principles in all our affairs."

In my earliest attempts at sobriety before I attended AA, I could go cold turkey and dry out without help. I had been conditioned to believe in the Trinity of a Godhead-the Father, Son and Holy Spirit from my childhood, but in the depth of my despair, anxiety and depression, that concept of God did not seem to be working for me. God was not answering my prayers, no matter how much I cried out for help to the cosmos.

I had suffered trauma as a child, witnessing, at age four, the death of a blood relative who was only fourteen years old. Later, I suffered the pain of losing my best friend, who drowned at fourteen while we were at the beach together; this suffering in my heart never left me. Soon enough there after my father drowned in an accident, and the great tragedy of all that I still endured was the suicide of my second eldest son at age twenty-six t years.

In hindsight, I now feel that God was present even though I could not see nor feel His presence. Signs in nature were revealed to me, like walking the beach and watching dolphins rounding up fish for a meal. It reminded me of rounding up cattle for the market on horseback in my former life in the bush. Other times, things would happen as another reminder as I looked out to sea and saw a whale breach so close to the beach that you could see the barnacles on its underbelly. Another time, resting against a tree in the bush, I found a giant snake asleep at my feet.

These now were symbolic signs of God in nature from the light, not the darkness I found myself in. The dark side had its influences, too—a crow landing nearby who seemed to be influencing my mood. I had spoken to it in no uncertain terms to go away as I knew it came from the dark, not the light. Without so much as a by your leave, it would fly off as my mood lifted but soon returned when I fell into the darkness again.

Soon, I found no solace in God but in nature. However, the God of my Christian upbringing seemed to have abandoned me, and I soon found that I had no faith at all.

In the Twelve Steps and Twelve Traditions of AA. Page 28 it states:

[Obviously, the dilemma of the wanderer from faith is that of profound confusion. He thinks himself lost to the comfort of any conviction at all. He cannot attain, even a small degree, the assurance of the believer, the agnostic, or the atheist. He is the bewildered one.]

"More than most people, I think, alcoholics want to know who they are, what this life is about, whether they have a divine origin and an appointed destiny, and whether there is a system of cosmic justice and love.

It is the experience of many of us in the early stages of drinking to feel that we have had glimpses of the Absolute and a heightened feeling of identification with the cosmos. While these glimpses and feelings doubtless have validity, they are deformed and finally swept away in the chemical, spiritual, and emotional damage wrought by alcoholism. In A.A., and many religious approaches, alcoholics find a great deal more of what they merely glimpsed and felt while trying to grope their way toward God in alcohol." (As Bill sees it, Page 323).

The Irish poet John O'Donohue's most famous quote resonates with me now more than any other: "May you recognise in your life the presence, power, and light of your soul. May you realise that you are never alone, that your soul in its brightness and belonging connects you intimately with the universe's rhythm."

God seemed to find his way to me before I came to believe through the Steps of AA. In my despair and loss of confidence in God, I was given a glimpse of the spiritual awakening in my first hospitalisation for alcoholism and depression. I had long since returned to the city to find work but instead booked myself into rehab, looking for a cure to my dilemma.

The resident psychiatrist I visited for 15 minutes every Friday was part of the deal with being a live-in patient. I remember telling him that I was lost, had no feelings of worldly direction, no contact with God and was stumbling around in a dark place. In his wisdom, he said: "Welcome to the beginning of your spiritual journey. I could have shot him on the spot. He recommended journaling my thoughts and feelings daily, listening to the sounds of silence, eating and resting even more than I was then doing. In time, It proved a godsend as I slowly recovered.

So, I decided to walk the Camino de Santiago. On that first pilgrimage, a lotus flower of creative ideas came from the well of feelings within me, and I began to write a daily journal of everything that happened in the 24 hours before. On my return, it proved to be the basis of a book of poetry, my first novel and an album of songs that welled up as a consequence. So it was that over the next decade, I returned to walk the Camino three times and continued to write books and songs, all of which have been published.

CHAPTER 6.

WILLING TO BELIEVE

I had come to a side of myself that I had not planned nor expected to come to light. In my AA programme, I came to believe in God again, but it was the reconnection with the belief of old that I was using as the template for my belief and practice of the steps of the programme. I had taken the logical, linear half-brain noting of the traditional faith of my Father's holy faith and applied it as I saw it for the next decade. I had deluded myself into believing that it was the way to go at the time. Then, I drank again one evening on my third Camino but did not continue. Fortunately, the previous ten years of attending three meetings of AA a week, prayer and meditation, and a mantra I had often chanted were the catalysts to stopping the drinking. I had been away from my spiritual programme for six weeks, walking in Spain and Ireland, not venturing to pray or even think about God. The saving grace was the long-term habit of the AA programme was enough for me to hear in my head, " Doug, you can't continue to drink."

It has been eight years now since I had that drink. Returning to the AA programme, I sort an answer to my God link. I had researched all I could find within the Bible, ancient scrolls, and Roman history, proving that Christ existed on this earth. In conclusion, I came to believe that Christ once walked this earth. However, it was not enough for me. So I concluded that if he had died on the cross for humanity to save us as had been told in the New Testament, and was raised from the dead and ascended into heaven, the answer for me was a belief in a power greater than

self must be in my imagination of a manifested Christ. So, I overlooked the logical, linear view favouring this, which manifested
for a long time.

However, it soon became apparent that if I combined my logical
brain with my creative imagination, God would become an 'Infinite Intelligence' who ran the show, not Doug.

The often-said statement in AA about our inward spiritual
journey is ' progress, not perfection.' When we come to believe
within the bounds of the AA programme, we realise that our
purpose in remaining sober is to fit ourselves to be of maximum service to God and the people around us. Of course, having a concept of a God of our understanding is more than help-
ful to be guided by, not just the programme's steps.

In Chinese symbolism, the yin and yang symbol (or taiji)
shows a balance between two opposites infused with a por-
tion of each element in each other. They are the two great
opposite but complementary forces at work in the cosmos.
Yin is represented as the female. Cold, dark, passive power and
yang represent masculinity, light and warmth. Earth, rain, soft,
evil, black, petite, even (numbers) are yin; heaven, sunshine,
hard, good, white, large, and odd are yang.

My concept of God was similar to yin-yang symbolism. I had infused a balance between the logical and creative minds and called
it the God of my understanding, but this proved to be an illusion
in time.

It was that I came to believe in the power of the third person of the Trinity as the guiding force to my sobriety and how I could practice the steps of AA a day at a time. In defining this powerful force, I referred to the fact that Jesus Christ, the son of the living God or the Infinite Intelligence if you will, had suffered and died on the cross to give us the connection to the Godhead by the Holy Spirit which cannot be defined in words but only feels deep within us and professed in deeds. For the present, this representation of my Higher Power is adequate for my purpose. His, for in it, I need not define God but merely accept that The Spirit of his presence in my life guides and protects me in the directions I choose to take for my betterment and for those with whom I come in contact at his bidding.

Equally, I have discovered through many different styles of meditation, from conjuring up visional guidance to visualising the charkas of the body to chanting and repeating a mantra, that ultimately, I've come to listen to my breath, the in-and-out warmth and coolness of the air, and the rising and falling of my chest. This tends to relax me, and I confess that I do not do it enough, as I should, for the quiet of my soul.

We must humble ourselves before God in meditation and prayer. The best example of humility in prayer is the parable of the Pharisee and the tax collector (Luke 18: 9-14).

In this parable, a Pharisee and a tax collector prayed to the temple. The Pharisees prayed about how good he was, but the tax collector asked for God's mercy as he was a sinner. Jesus said that the tax collector who went home was justified before God.

He concluded, " Everyone who exalts himself shall be humbled, and he who humbles himself shall be exalted."

Tax collectors were hated in biblical times and were regarded as sinners. They were Jews who worked for the Romans, so this made them traitors. People resented paying taxes to the foreigners who ruled over them. The Romans did not pay tax collectors an actual wage. Instead, they were expected to take extra money and keep some for themselves. Many tax collectors were dishonest and abused this system by taking far too much.

Jesus wants to teach people the importance of praying with the right attitude. This parable is aimed at the Pharisees, who think they are righteous and look down on others. Jews had to pray three times a day, and people would go to the temple for private prayer.

The Pharisees stood up to pray, as was their custom. Then, they prayed about themselves, informing God of the wrong things they had not done: " I am not like other men—robbers, evil-doers, and adulterers." Then, they spoke about their religious practices, fasting twice weekly and giving tithes. The Pharisee thought he was praying, but the only person he was praising was himself.

On the other hand, the tax collector put his head down and kept hitting himself to show his sorry. He knew he had done wrong and needed God to forgive him. Nobody can be proud of himself in front of God.

The men went home, but only the tax collector pleased God, as he was humble and asked for forgiveness. A person's attitude is essential to God.

[More than most people, the alcoholic leads a double life. He is very much an actor. He presents his stage character to the outer world, Which he likes his fellows to see. He wants to enjoy a particular reputation but doesn't deserve it.

The inconsistency is made worse by the things he does on his see. Upon sobering up, specific episodes revolt him that he vaguely remembers. These memories are a nightmare. He trembles to think someone might have observed him. As fast as he can, he pushes these memories far inside himself. He hopes they will never see the light of day. He is under constant fear and tension-which makes for more drinking.] The aforementioned is an extract from The Big Book of Alcoholics Anonymous and serves to remind us of our hidden secrets whilst still drinking.

In our early sobriety, we may find it hard to share our past with another human being. Then, it serves us well to find a place to sit quietly and illuminate every dark corner of the past. We need to withhold nothing. We can be alone and at perfect peace. We then begin to feel the nearness of our Creator. We may have been conditioned to certain spiritual beliefs, but now we begin to have a spiritual experience. The feeling that the drinking problem has disappeared will often come strongly. We feel we are on the broad highway, walking hand in hand with the Universal Spirit. Sometimes, events may cause one to be on the brink of despair before a turnaround. It took a series of tragic circumstances and materially tricky experiences before I came out the other side. In hindsight, I was a hard nut for God to crack, and it now seems as a sober alcoholic that the path I trod through the night of the soul was not unlike the trail of Job. Unlike Job, I lost faith in God for some time, but it all worked out through the healing power of God and the AA programme.

I had a dream run financially for over a decade. Whatever I touched turned to gold, and my family reaped the rewards of my success. Then, everyone turned pear-shaped one winter morning when I got a phone call from my youngest son advising that my then-wife had left with another man and cleaned the house out of our mutual possessions. Divorce followed, and the settlement of material possessions was divided, but not without a court battle over the next year. The family moved on, leaving me with the pieces to pick up again. Friends turned against me, and I felt all alone, desperately holding on to the business of making money primarily to fund solicitors' fees at the time. The business market at the time was undergoing a drastic change, too. The previous year, I had forty casual employees, and this soon dropped over the following years to just ten; then, finally, there was just me trying in my alcoholic state of mind to hold it all together.

During the worst of my despair, I increased my daily drinking, not realising that I was already drinking alcoholically. Then another phone call. It was the police wanting me to identify the body of a friend who was on his way to stay with me for a few days to support me in my misery and had a heart attack and died. The phone continued to ring with bad news. Another friend had committed suicide, and within two weeks, a call from overseas that my second eldest son had committed suicide. I went from bad to worse, and the drinking continued day and night. I went from despair to deep depression, extreme anxiety and suicidal thoughts.

There was no way I could cope with the business, so I opened the door to allow my inventory to be taken by charities. I could have put it all into storage but reasoned it best to let it all go and walk away. It proved to be the right thing to do in the long run, even though I felt the pride possessions I had built over the previous decade were being extracted from me. The eagles moved in for the pickings, followed by a team of locus who fed on the crumbs.

For a time, I went cold turkey off the drink but returned to the drink once again when I started to recover. There, I attended regular meetings of AA and learned about the steps of the program. Like all in the fellowship, I had a long reconstruction ahead of me, and it's still happening.

As the Big Book of Alcoholics Anonymous states in chapter 6, Into Action: [It is easy to let up on the **spiritual program of action** and rest on our laurels. We are headed for trouble if we do, for alcohol is a subtle foe. We are not cured of alcoholism. What we have is a daily reprieve contingent on the maintenance of our spiritual condition. Every day, we must carry the vision of God's will into all our activities." How can I best serve Thee_ **Thy will not mine be done.** These are thoughts that must go with us constantly. We can exercise our willpower along this line if we wish. It is the proper use of the will.]

As laid out in chapter 6 of the Big Book of Alcoholics Anonymous, alcoholics who stay sober and work the Twelve Steps will see these Promises come true: We are going to find new freedom and new happiness. We will not regret the past nor wish to shut the door on it. We will comprehend the word serenity. We will know peace. No matter how far down the scale we have gone, we will see how our experience can benefit others. The feeling of uselessness and self-pity will disappear. We will lose interest in selfish things and gain interest in our fellows. Self-seeking will slip away. Our whole attitude and outlook upon life will change. Fear of people and economic insecurity will leave us. We will intuitively know how to handle situations that used to baffle us. We will suddenly realise that God is doing what we could not do for ourselves.

The Big Book's promises mostly describe the change in attitude that will transpire within the alcoholic, " sometimes quickly, and sometimes slowly." They may take time, but they "will always materialise if we work for them."

A person working a good program to recover from alcoholism will surely experience an internal shift that [produces a new level of peace and well-being. What represents the central benefits are freedom, happiness, peace, and serenity, as well as the gift of being of service and benefit to others. Simultaneously, the Big Book promises the departure of the unwelcome by-products of the alcoholic. Fear, regret, uselessness, self-pity, selfishness, and self-seeking leave us forever. There are essentials for the recovering alcoholic to abide by: The recovering alcoholic is guided by the program, the Big Book, the Twelve Steps and their instructions.

The final source of wisdom comes from within: the recovering alcoholic must create a hopeful vision of the future and be determined to make it occur.

The fourth source of guidance, the self, is why the Promises of the Big Book are so important. They precisely describe the alcoholic. They precisely describe for the alcoholic the bright future that lies ahead for anyone who commits to recovery, and they assure the alcoholic of a sober life hereafter as an outcome.

The recovering alcoholic establishes a relationship with a Higher Power, whatever its form, and trusts in the guidance of the Spirit. So it is that one enters into the spiritual habits of living a day at a time as a sober alcoholic. However, it's more about implementing the lessons learned along the way. In time, we begin to feel the Spirit enter us. In this, we have become God-conscious. We have started to develop this vital sixth sense. It is then that we go further, which means more action. We have God in our lives through the steps.

So it is then that we enact the eleventh Step of AA in our daily habits; " Sought through prayer and meditation to improve a constant contact with God as we understood Him, praying only for knowledge of his will for us and the power to carry that out. "

In my early sobriety, while I still had the desire for alcohol, I often repeated as a mantra the Serenity prayer, which is the opening and closing prayer at all AA meetings: " God grant me the Serenity to accept the things I cannot change, have the courage to change the things I can, and the wisdom to know the difference." The desire for alcohol left me like a miracle after six months in the programme. It was a daily habit to meditate and pray, and it kept me sober a day at a time. Except for a one evening slip after ten years of practising the Steps, I drank again; I had not mediated nor prayed b, been to meetings or thought about God for six weeks. I've been back on the straight-and-narrow AA path again as a sober alcoholic for eight years now and find meditation and prayer an essential part of my sobriety and peace of mind.

Some alcoholics entirely repeat the St. Francis Prayer as a reminder of our duty in life.

'God, make me an instrument of your peace; where there is hatred, let me sow love; where there is injury, pardon, doubt, faith, darkness light, and where there is sadness, joy. Grant that I not so much seek to be consoled as to console, to be understood, to understand, to be loved as to love. For it is giving that we receive, pardoning that we are pardoned and dying that we are born to eternal life."

Some sober alcoholics like to pray as they relate to each AA Step. Here they are for your consideration:

First Step Prayer

: Dear Lord,

I admit that I am powerless over my addiction.

I acknowledge that my life is unmanageable when I try to control it.

Help me this day to understand

The true meaning of powerlessness.

Remove from me all denial of my addiction.

Second Step Prayer

Heavenly Father,

I know only you can restore me to sanity.

I humbly ask that you remove all twisted thoughts &

Addictive behaviour from me this day.

Heal my spirit & restore in me a clear mind.

Third Step Prayer

God,

I offer myself to Thee.

To build with me & to do with me as Thou wilt.

Relieve me of the bondage of self, that I may better do Thy will.

Take away my difficulties,

That victory over them may bear witness.

To those I would help of Thy Power,

Thy love & Thy way of life,

May I do Thy will always!

Fourth Step Prayer

: Dear God,

I have made my life a mess.

I have done it, but I cannot undo it.

My mistakes are mine &

I will begin a searching & fearless moral inventory.

I will write down my wrongs.

But I will also include that which is good.

I pray for the strength to complete the task.

Fifth Step Prayer

Almighty God, my inventory has shown me who I am. I admit to my wrongs, yet I ask for Your help admitting them to another person and You. Assure and be with me in this step; without it, I cannot progress in my recovery. With Your help, I can do this. Amen.

Sixth Step Prayer

Dear God,

I am ready for Your help.

I have removed the defects of character

from me, which I now realise are obstacles to my recovery.

Please help me to continue being honest with myself &

Guide me toward spiritual & mental health.

Seventh Step Prayer

: My Creator,

I am now willing that you should have all of me, good & bad.

I pray that you now remove from me every single defect of character.

Grant me strength as I leave here to do your bidding.

Eighth Step Prayer

Higher Power,

I ask for your help in making my list of all those I have harmed.

I will take responsibility for my mistakes &

Be forgiving to others as You are forgiving to me.

Please grant me the willingness to begin my restitution.
God, I pray.

Ninth Step Prayer

Higher Power:
I pray for the right attitude to make my amends,
and I am always mindful not to harm others.
I ask for Your guidance in making indirect amends.
Most important, I will continue to make amends.
By staying abstinent and helping others &
We are growing in spiritual progress.

Tenth Step Prayer

I pray I may continue:
To grow in understanding & effectiveness;
To take daily spot-check inventories of myself;
To correct mistakes when I make them;
To take responsibility for my actions;
To be ever aware of my negative &
Self-defeating attitudes & behaviours;
To keep my wilfulness in check;
Always remember I need Your help;
To keep love & tolerance of others as my code; &
To continue in daily prayer how I can best serve You,
My Higher Power.

Eleventh Step Prayer

Higher Power, as I understand You,
I pray to keep my connection with You.
Open & clear from the confusion of daily life.
Through my prayers & meditation, I ask especially for

I want to be accessible and follow your spiritual path. I pray for the guidance of correct thought and positive action. You will not mine be done.

When we have completed Steps 1 to 11, our lives have reached a level where we apply the Steps to our daily lives and actively set out to help the still-suffering alcoholic. This is where Step 12 comes into play.

Twelfth Step Prayer

Dear God,
My spiritual awakening continues to unfold.
The help I have received I shall pass on & give to others,
Both in & out of the Fellowship.
For this opportunity, I am grateful.
I humbly pray to continue walking daily—the way of spiritual progress.

It is through these Steps of AA and our Higher Power that we alcoholics stay sober a day at a time.

CHAPTER 7.

WHAT'S NEXT?

It is a personal preference as to the routine and type of meditative practice one undertakes daily. It depends upon one's state of mind during the training. That is why taking a few minutes to relax before meditating is a good idea. Closing your eyes and scanning the body from head to toe is an excellent way to start the practice. Whilst some may prefer listening to music, chanting a mantra or visual imagery, focusing on the breath is most beneficial. I like reading spiritual material before meditation, like AA's Daily Reflection. It's a matter of choice, and you may want to try many types of meditative practice before you settle on the one best suited to your purpose.

The 12th Step: " Having had a spiritual awakening as a result of these steps, we tried to carry this message to alcoholics and to practice these principles in all our affairs."

The fellowship of AA is second to none in supporting fellow alcoholics (and addicts) to stay clean and sober one day at a time. Once the 12 Steps are ingrained in your life, you are on autopilot as it were to helping other alcohols obtain sobriety. The spiritual experience one comes to accept is a gift that cannot be explained, for no matter how much you do to help another, you receive and maintain a spiritual gift from God that never ceases. It's the best method I know for remaining clean and sober.

Step 12 asks Alcoholics Anonymous members to apply the guiding principles of the 12-step program in every aspect of their lives. It also asks members to help others who are still suffering to achieve sobriety by sharing their experiences and giving other alcoholics hope and strength. This service to others is paramount because, without it, Alcoholics Anonymous would not exist.

Most people take about 90 days to do all the 12 Steps of Alcoholics Anonymous. However, it is not unusual to take more than 90 days. Attending meetings is paramount to sobriety.

The 12-step programs of Alcoholics Anonymous can be very beneficial in helping you heal from the mental health impact of substance abuse and the transition to sober living. The 12 steps help you face the problem, surrender to a higher power, increase self-awareness, and build self-esteem and self-acceptance. AA Twelve Step programs offer support and acceptance from a loving, non-judgmental community. As an AA member, the social support you receive through sponsorships and meetings can play a vital role in helping you stay clean. Moreover, the 12 steps often help to rebuild relationships with loved ones, but most definitely develop a support network for the future.

The peer support, encouragement, and accountability offered by Alcoholics Anonymous can help you overcome addiction and stay sober. Continued AA attendance benefits many people and helps them stay sober forever.

AA meetings take place in various formats. Generally, they involve members talking about their drinking and the actions they took to stop drinking. In-person meetings typically occur in churches, recreational centres, clubhouses, treatment centres, and office buildings. Some take place in outdoor settings such as parks and beaches. Online meetings may have a video on or off.

A standard meeting format involves a leader or chair selecting a topic for discussion. Speakers share their experiences with alcohol. The typical format is "What was I like before alcohol? What happened to trigger alcohol use?" "What am I like now?" Many AA groups devote one or more weekly meetings to the Big Book and 12 Steps, focusing on studying each step by rotation. After the meeting, people may introduce themselves and socialise.

Most people who have participated in an addiction treatment program have been exposed to the 12 Steps in some manner or form. However, to truly get the maximum benefit from the 12 Steps of Alcoholics Anonymous, you need to immerse yourself in the steps. You can accomplish this by going to AA meetings regularly. Hearing the experiences of others will give you strength and confidence.

I had been discussing the workings of Professor William James, an American theologian known as a modern father of philosophy. Not to be confused with his son, the novelist Henry James Jr., nor the writings of his daughter Alice James. In his younger years, Professor James prepared an edition of Robert Sandeman's 'Let-

ters on Theron and Aspasio,' called the principal literary docu-
ment of a Scottish sect that opposed the Presbyterian Church.
Sandeman called his work "a far more faithful exhibition of
Gospel truth than any other work."

What specifically interested James was its radically egalitarian
message. For Sandman wrote."The whole New Testament speaks
aloud that as to the matter of acceptance with God, there is no
difference between one man and another - no difference between
the best-accomplished gentleman and the most infamous
scoundrel; no difference between the most virtuous lady and the
vilest of prostitutes…" In his work investigating spirituality, he
befriended Ralph Waldo Emerson but found little satisfaction in
his spiritual philosophy. Likewise, the atheist viewpoints of
Thomas Carlyle, to whom he was introduced via Emerson. Henry
James found his spiritual home in Emanuel Swedenborg, the
Swedish scientist, religious visionary, and teacher. He held most
of the leading writers of his time in low regard, with the possible
exception of Walt Whitman and Henry David Thoreau. I used
Whitman's comment on pilgrimage in a PowerPoint presentation
on 'What is a Pilgrimage and why do it?' In his remarks of Pilgrims in a world of seekers, Walt quotes, " Not I…or anyone else,
can travel that road for you. You must travel it yourself," I also
related to Thoreau's two famous quotes: " The masses of men
lead lives of quiet desperation" and: "Every man's heart beats to
the tune of a different drummer, let him follow the drummer that
he hears." But I digress from James' path of working through his
spiritual crisis by following Swedenborg's words in stages. He
had his way of expressing it: "The curse of mankind, that which
keeps our manhood so little and so depraved, is the sense of self-

hood, and the absurd abominable opinion of ego it engenders."
He remained attached to Swedenborg's works for the rest of his
life and travelled extensively, devoted to lecturing on the doctrine
and writing copious volumes on the subject matter. He wrote a
complex 400-page compendium, 'A Variety of Religious Experiences.' It is interesting to note that Bill Wilson of AA fame, in his
research of the Oxford Group and his mission into the spiritual
conscience, discovered this 400-page work of James and con-
densed it down to just three steps on the path to spirituality. Bill
Wilson stated that Man first experiences a calamity from which
there is no turning back. Next follows a mental and or spiritual
collapse that there seems to be no way out, and finally, there is a
cry out for a Higher power to help, usually via prayer.

[Deep down in every man, woman, and child is the fundamental idea of God. It may be obscured by calamity, by
pomp, by the worship of other things, but in some form or
different, it is there. Faith in a Power greater than ourselves
and miraculous demonstrations of that Power in human lives
are facts as old as man himself.] (As Bill See It. Page 152.)

"Faith may often be given through inspired teaching or a con-
vincing personal example of its fruits. It may sometimes be had
through reason. For instance, many clergy members believe St.
Thomas Aquinas proved God's existence by sheer logic. But what
can one do when all these channels fail? As such was my griev-
ous dilemma.

"It was when I came fully to believe I was powerless over alcohol, only when I appealed to God, who just might exist, that I ex-

perienced a spiritual awakening. This freedom-giving experience came first, and faith followed afterwards–a gift indeed!" (Alcoholics Anonymous Pg 55)

So the man who simplistically summarise the essence of William James' complex thesis on spirituality had determined what makes for progress in belief in God was by calamity, collapse and a cry for help to a Higher Power. Here is a brief of his story and what transpired to turn a non-believer to accept a God of his understanding and co-found Alcoholics Anonymous to benefit the suffering alcoholic.

Bill Wilson was one of the many young military officers from Pittsburg who was made to feel heroic on his homecoming. Bill W was a twenty-two-year-old veteran of foreign wars who had experienced love, applause, war, and moments sublime, and there, he had discovered alcohol. He had proved himself a leader of men in his regiment and imagined one day being the head of vast enterprises he would manage with great skill. There were no limits to his ambitions, and soon, he was employed as an investigator for a surety company. He began studying law at night school, and the drive to success soon overtook him.

Bill married Lois Burnham, his long-time girlfriend, on January 24, 1918, just before he left to serve in WW1 as a 2nd lieutenant in the Coast Artillery. After his military service, he returned to live with his wife in New York. He failed to graduate from law school because he was too drunk to pick up his diploma. Wilson became a stock speculator and successfully travelled the country with his wife, evaluating companies for potential investors. Lois had a hidden agenda: she hoped the travel would keep Wilson from drinking. However, Wilson's constant drinking made business impossible and ruined his reputation.

A decade of heavy drinking was taking its toll. In 1933, Wilson was committed to the Hospital for Drug and Alcohol Addictions in New York City four times under the care of Doctor William Silkworth. Silkworth's theory was that alcoholism was a matter of both physical and mental control: a craving, the manifestation of a physical allergy (the physical inability to stop drinking once started), and an obsession with the mind (to take the first drink). Wilson gained hope from Silkworth's assertion that alcoholism was a medical condition, but even that knowledge could not help him. He was eventually told that he would either die from his alcoholism or have to be locked up permanently due to what was commonly referred to as a "wet brain".

In November 1934, an old drinking companion, Eddy Thacher, visited Wilson. Wilson was astounded to find Thacher had been sober for weeks under the guidance of the evangelical Christians known as the Oxford Group. Wilson took some interest in the group, but shortly after Thacher's visit, he was again admitted to Towns Hospital to recover from a bout of drinking. It was his fourth and last stay at Towns under Silkworth's care, and he showed signs of delirium tremens. There, Bill W had a "White Light" spiritual experience and quit drinking. Earlier that evening, Thacher had visited and tried to persuade him to turn himself over to the care of a Christian deity who would liberate him from alcohol. He was also given a belladonna, which causes hallucinations. According to Wilson, while lying in bed, depressed and despairing, he cried out, "I'll do anything! Anything at all! If there be a God, let Him show Himself!" He then had the sensation of a bright light, a feeling of ecstasy, and a new serenity. He never drank again for the rest of his life. Wilson described his experience to Silkworth, who said, "Something has happened to you I don't understand. But you had better hang on to it."

Wilson joined the Oxford Group and tried to help other alcoholics. They did not get sober, but Wilson kept sober himself. During a failed business trip to Akron, Ohio, Wilson was tempted to drink again and decided that to remain sober, he needed to help another alcoholic. He called phone numbers in a church directory and eventually secured an introduction to Doctor Bob Smith, an alcoholic Oxford Group member. Wilson explained Silkworth's theory that alcoholics suffer from a physical allergy and a mental obsession. Wilson shared that the only way he was able to stay sober was through having had a spiritual experience. Smith was familiar with the tenets of the Oxford Group and, upon hearing of Wilson's experience, "began to pursue the spiritual remedy for his malady with a willingness that he had never before been able to muster. After a brief relapse, he sobered, never to drink again..." Wilson and Smith began working with other alcoholics. After that summer in Akron, Wilson returned to New York, where he started having success helping alcoholics in what they called "a nameless squad of drunks" in an Oxford Group there.

In 1938, after about 100 alcoholics in Akron and New York had become sober, the 'fellowship' decided to promote its program of recovery through the publication of a book, for which Wilson was chosen as the primary author. The book was named Alcoholics

Anonymous and included a list of suggested activities for spiritual growth known as the Twelve Steps. The movement itself took on the name of the book. Bill incorporated the principles of nine of the Twelve Traditions (a set of spiritual guidelines to ensure the survival of individual AA groups) in his foreword to the original edition; later, Traditions One, Two, and Ten were specified when all twelve statements were published. The AA General Service conference of 1955 was a landmark event for Wilson, and he turned over the leadership of the maturing organisation to an elected board.

1939 Wilson and fellow alcoholic Marty Mann visited High Watch Farm in Kent, CT. They would go on to found what is now High Watch Recovery Centre, the world's first alcohol and addiction recovery centre founded on Twelve Step principles. Bill Wilson strongly advocated that AA groups have not the "slightest reform or political complexion".In 1946, he wrote, "No AA group or members should ever, in such a way as to implicate AA, express any opinion on outside controversial issues – particularly those of politics, alcohol reform or sectarian religion. The Alcoholics Anonymous groups oppose no one. Concerning such matters, they can express no views whatsoever." Reworded, this became AA's "Tradition 10".

During the 1950s, Bill began a fifteen-year affair with Helen Wynn, a woman who was 18 years his junior, whom he met through AA. There were reports of his further womanising, but despite this, he stayed true to his spiritual belief in a higher power and AA. Bill W wrote numerous books on spirituality and sobriety, building up quite a legacy for those who had an addiction.

Wilson arranged in 1963 to leave 10% of his book royalties to Helen Wynn and the rest to his wife, Lois. Bill W was no saint, and his experimentation with LSD for mental stability and later reports of the use of Vitamin B3 for depression and anxiety are well recorded.

During the last years of his life, Wilson rarely attended AA meetings to avoid being asked to speak as the co-founder rather than as an alcoholic. A heavy smoker, Wilson eventually suffered from emphysema and later pneumonia. He continued to smoke while dependent on an oxygen tank in the late 1960s. The cruel irony is that in his final months of living, his desire for alcohol returned, but he did not drink and remained abstinent for the remaining sober of his days. Bill W had been sober 37 years when he passed.

CHAPTER 8.

SPIRITUAL WISDOM

Augustine of Hippo, the North African bishop of the fourth and fifth centuries *anno Domini* and author of the famous *Confessions* and *The City of God,* continues to be perhaps the most critical post-biblical theologian of Christian thought. Augustine believed that most people lived lives like his own despite their apparent differences in time, space, and detail.

He felt his story was not unique but an example of struggling, discontented human beings earnestly looking for lasting happiness—just like we are! He wandered about in ignorance and confusion, trying to figure out what life was all about—just like we do! He attached himself in love helter-skelter to those things he thought would make him happy—just like us! He discovered that the satisfaction he derived from the things he loved for happiness didn't last very long—just as the satisfaction we derive from the things we love doesn't last very long for us, either!

Augustine also realised how his ongoing, excessive dependence upon various entities to secure the fulfilment he was looking for enslaved him in a miserable life of bad habits and virtual addictions. Sex was Augustine's specific downfall. His intense quest for contentment resulted in nothing but failure and frustration. His experience echoed that of the "preacher" in the book of Ecclesiastes: "Then I considered all that my hands had done and the toil I had expended in doing it, and behold, all was vanity and a striving after wind, and there was nothing to be gained under the sun." (2:11) No matter how hard he tried, Augustine still felt empty, depressed, and restless. Sound familiar?

However, after a long, bumpy ride, Augustine finally discovered that God had made him and all of us for himself and that his heart and all human hearts will be forever restless (that is, unhappy) until they rest in Him. Augustine tells the story of himself, warts and all, in his famed spiritual autobiography, *Confessions*.

As one of the Church's great classics, Augustine no doubt wrote his *Confessions* to acknowledge his faith in God as his chief good and out of a need to confess his sins before Him. But I think he also had other purposes in mind for this work. Since he believed there was something about himself as a human being and his journey that was typical of almost everyone, everywhere, he also wrote this book to assist us in our journeys toward God and genuine happiness—hopefully saving us considerable agony and disappointment—by the example of his own life. His loves and his life were disordered without God; his loves and his life were re-ordered in God. His example consists of an education of the heart in God, in love, and authentic happiness. You, me, Augustine—indeed, we are here and all in this together.

Augustine's world is both pre-print and pre-literate. It emerged from a fundamentally oral culture where the rhetor reigns and the bishop's legacy is his sermons, not his books. Finally, Augustine's "world" is relatively small, circumscribed by the empire's boundaries. What could such a foreign voice say in our postmodern, post-Christian, post-literate, globalised world?

Augustine's voice continues to loom over our imaginations—indeed, it continues to fuel them. While some still enjoy railing against caricatures of Augustine the misogynist or Augustine the "substance metaphysician," a steady stream of thinkers in the twentieth century and into the present have found in the vast expanse of Augustine's thought a catalyst for naming "the present" and understanding ourselves. I engage him head-on; he accompanies me in my engagements with the world.

First, contrary to some ghastly, puritan "textbook" picture of Augustine, when I think of the tireless bishop, I think first and foremost of love. For Augustine, love is what we are. We are made to love, for love, and what we love defines us. In 'confessions', he wrote: " Our hearts are restless until we rest in you." In ' The City of God' he defines "people" as " the association of a multitude of rational beings united by a common agreement on the objects of their love." This view is in contrast to the rationalism we inherited from modernity. I have found Augustine's emphasis on love to be a more holistic account of what drives us. Second, while Augustine contends that all humans are essentially lovers, he also recognises that we don't all love the same thing. Indeed, the Fall, rather than shutting down love or desire, disorders and misdirects us. We end up loving or "enjoying" what we should only be "using;" in short, we start making idols out of creation when, in fact, they're meant to function as icons that point us to God. But for Augustine, this isn't just a matter of intellectual mistakes. It comes down to how we construe the world—what we love and how we love it.

Finally, Augustine's political life account is incredibly nuanced and a rich resource for contemporary self-understanding. In particular, I appreciate two features of the *City of God*: first, he continues to make love central to what defines a "people" or "commonwealth"—that a *civitas* is determined by what it loves as "ultimate." Second, what we love is inextricably linked to what we worship. True justice is a matter of proper worship. Exploring that (essential) connection could reconfigure how we analyse our political institutions. Augustine gave us the perennial and pride (that probably says more about me than Augustine). Concerning the first two temptations, he recognises that he has acquired "some capacity for self-exploration." But when it comes to ambition? "In this matter, almost none" (10.37.60). Pride and ambition are sly tempters, easily parading as angels of light. *How can we live indifferent to the praise of others?* He asks. If we perform our calling well, we shall receive praise. Shall we be negligent in avoiding the temptation of praise? Hardly. One can see how the very project of writing his *Confession* totters on the cusp of this tension. "So why are you writing the *Confessions*?" Augustine is asking himself. With unflinching honesty, Augustine analyses his prideful inclinations that would be almost torturous if not suffused with grace. And this from the bishop!

While they announce that Augustine once was lost and is now found, they also admit that even those who are found sometimes feel lost—that "I Still Haven't Found What I'm Looking For" can be the anthem of Christians, too.

NEWS OF ANTHONY OF EGYPT, especially his sacrificial solitude, spread widely long before he died. At Rome, Marcella, a wealthy noblewoman already widowed at age 17, heard about him around 340 and, in response, turned her mansion into an ascetic community devoted to prayer and Bible study. Other Roman matrons followed her pioneering example.

But when Athanasius, who had told Marcella about Antony, put Antony's story down in writing, Antony's influence became more extraordinary still. As Athanasius told his readers at the beginning of his *Life of Antony*, "I feel that, once you have heard the story, you will not merely admire the man but will wish to emulate his commitment as well."

Within a decade of publication, a Latin version (Athanasius wrote *Life* in Greek) had been published, and a copy was given to two Roman officials in Trier, a prosperous regional centre in what is now part of Germany.

 As one ancient account records, "One of them began to read it and was amazed and set on fire. The Roman official was filled with holy love and sobering shame. Angry with himself, he turned his eyes to his friend and said, ' Tell me, I beg you, what do we hope to achieve with all our labours? What is our aim in life? Can we hope for any higher office in the palace than to be friends of the emperor? If I wish to become God's friend, in an instant, I may become that now.' "

After experiencing an inner conversion, he returned to the book in turmoil. "I have decided to serve God," he said, "and I propose to start doing that from this hour in this place." His companion joined him in this resolve. Soon, wives followed suit, vowing themselves to ascetic abstinence.

This dramatic story comes from Ponticianus, who told it in the mid-380s to Augustine, an imperial official in Milan. Ponticianus was a high imperial official, an African (like Augustine), and a baptised Christian believer (unlike Augustine).

He was surprised one day to find Augustine and his friend Alypius reading Paul's letters. As they talked, Ponticianius told them about Antony of Egypt and his extraordinary life—and discovered with astonishment that Augustine and Alypius had never heard of Antony nor "the flocks in the monasteries and their manner of life well pleasing to God and the fertile deserts of the wilderness."

As Politicians spoke, Augustine, just like the civil servants in Trier, was "violently overcome by a fearful sense of shame." The intellectual arguments that might have kept him from following these humbling examples had all been exhausted. Dare he face liberation from "the treadmill of habit?" In the heat of passion, his words to Alypius, as Augustine later put it in his *Confessions*, "said less about the state of my mind than my brow, cheeks, eyes, colour and tone of voice."

They went into the garden, where Augustine's soul struggles raged on until he heard a child's voice telling him, "Take up and read." He remembered Antony's decisive response to an apparently chance hearing of the words of Jesus, "Go sell all you have ... and come, follow me" (Matt. 19:21). For Augustine, it was Romans 13:13-14 as Paul's letter fell open: "Put on the Lord Jesus Christ and make no provision for the lusts of the flesh." Augustine's conversion to Christianity was inseparable from his commitment to a life of ascetic discipline. As we have discovered in the previous chapter, Augustine, through his 'Confessions' and " City of God' sermons, would become the greatest theologian in the church for the next 1,000 years.

Athanasius's purpose in writing Antony's *Life* had gained tremendous success. **Anthony of Egypt** was a religious hermit and one of the earliest Desert Fathers. He is considered the founder and father of organised Christian monasticism. His rule (book of observances) represented one of the first attempts to codify guidelines for monastic living.

A disciple of St. Paul of Thebes, Anthony began to practice an ascetic life at the age of 20 and, after 15 years, withdrew for absolute solitude to a mountain by the Nile called Pispir (now Dayr al-Maymūn), where he lived from about 286 to 305. During this retreat, he began his legendary combat against the devil, withstanding a series of temptations famous in Christian theology and iconography. At about 305, Anthony emerged from his retreat to instruct and organise the monastic life of the hermits who imitated him and had established themselves nearby. When Christian persecution ended after the Edict of Milan (313), he moved to a mountain in the Eastern Desert, between the Nile and the Red, where the monastery Dayr Mārī Antonios still stands. There he remained, receiving visitors and occasionally crossing the desert to Pispir. He ventured twice to Alexandria, the last time (c. 350), to preach against Arianism, a heretical doctrine teaching that Christ the Son is not of the same substance as God the Father.

The early monks who followed Anthony into the desert considered themselves the vanguard of God's army, and by fasting and performing other ascetic practices, they attempted to attain the same state of spiritual purity and freedom from temptation that they saw realised in Anthony. Anthony's spiritual combats with what he envisioned as the forces of evil made his life one long struggle against the Devil. According to St. Athanasius, the bishop of Alexandria, the Devil's assault on Anthony took the form of visions, either seductive or horrible, experienced by the saint. For example, at times, the Devil appeared in the guise of a monk bringing bread during his fasts or in the form of wild beasts, women, or soldiers, sometimes beating the saint and leaving him in a deathly state. Anthony endured many such attacks, and those who witnessed them were convinced they were real. Every vision conjured up by Satan was repelled by Anthony's fervent prayer and penitential acts.

The life of St. Anthony of Egypt confirms Robinson Crusoe's mode of living on his desert island, which became the prototype of the lonely man living in paradise. He sought to distance himself from classical Christian ideals and explore his spiritual origins. Anthony preferred to live as a society in the desert in Egypt rather than submit to the coercive nature of the imperial edict. To him, the rise of the state was the diminishing of humanity itself.

Long before St. Anthony and his religious awakening, the father of all ascetic monks who ventured into the desert to find himself or at least a place of isolation far from the madding crowd was one Paul of Thebes, also known as Paul the Hermit or Paul the Anchorite who lived between c. 227 – c. 341, he was considered a saint by the Catholic Church, Eastern Orthodox religion, and Oriental Christian Churchs. Paul of Thebes was born around 227 in the Thebaid of Egypt. Paul and his married sister lost their parents. His brother-in-law sought to betray him to the persecutors to obtain Paul's inheritance. According to Jerome's *Vitae Patrum* (*Vita Pauli primi eremitae*[8]), Paul fled to the Theban desert at age sixteen during the persecution of Valerians and Decius around AD 250. He was the inspiration for many a desert father to follow his lifestyle.

He lived in the mountains of this desert in a cave near a clear spring and a palm tree, the leaves of which provided him with clothing and the fruit of which provided him with his only source of food until he was 43 years old when a raven started bringing him half a loaf of bread daily. He would remain in that cave for almost a hundred years for the rest of his life.

Life of Anthony of the Desert: Most of what is known about Anthony comes from the *Life of Anthony*. Written in Greek c. 360 by Athanasius of Alexandria, it depicts Anthony as an illiterate and holy man who, through his existence in a primordial landscape, has an absolute connection to the divine truth, which is always in harmony with that of Athanasius as the biographer.

Anthony was born in Koma in Lower Egypt to wealthy landowner parents. When he was about 20 years old, his parents died and left him in the care of his unmarried sister. Shortly after, he followed the gospel exhortation in Matthew 19:21, "If you want to be perfect, go, sell what you have and give to the poor, and you will have treasures in heaven." Anthony gave away some of his family's lands to his neighbours, sold the remaining property, and donated the funds to people experiencing poverty. He then left to live an ascetic life, placing his sister with a group of Christian nuns.

Anthony remained in the area for the next fifteen years, spending the first years as the disciple of another local hermit. Various legends suggest that he worked as a swine-herder during this period. Anthony is sometimes considered the first monk and the first to initiate solitary desertification, but others were before him. In the 1st century AD, the Jewish philosopher Philo of Alexandria described ascetic hermits and loosely organised hermit communities as long established in the harsh environment of Lake Mareotis and other accessible regions.

Philo believed that "this class of persons may be met with in many places, for Greece and barbarian countries want to enjoy whatever is perfectly good." Christian ascetics such as Thecla had likewise retreated to isolated locations on the outskirts of cities. Anthony is notable for surpassing this tradition and heading to the desert proper. He left for the alkaline Desert on the edge of the Western desert about 95 km (59 mi) west of Alexandria. He remained there for 13 years.

Anthony maintained a rigorous ascetic diet. He ate only bread, salt and water and never meat or wine, eating at most only once daily and sometimes fasting for two or four days. According to Athanasius, the devil fought Anthony by afflicting him with boredom, laziness, and the phantoms of women, which he had overcome through the power of prayer, providing a theme for Christian art. After that, he moved to one of the tombs near his native village. There it was, the *Life* records those strange conflicts with demons in the shape of wild beasts, who inflicted blows upon him and sometimes left him nearly dead.

After fifteen years of this life, at the age of thirty-five, Anthony determined to withdraw from the habitations of men and retire in absolute solitude. He went into the desert to a mountain by the Nile called Pispil (now Der-el-Memun). He lived strictly enclosed in At times, pilgrims visited him, whom he refused to see, but gradually, several would-be disciples established themselves in caves and huts around the mountain.

Thus, a colony of ascetics was formed, and they begged Anthony to come forth and guide them in spiritual life. Eventually, he yielded to their importance and emerged from his retreat around 305. Surprisingly, he appeared not emaciated but healthy in mind and body.

CHAPTER 9.

THE JOURNEY INWARD

Anthony devoted himself to the instruction and organisation of the great monks growing up around him for five or six years. Still, in time, he once again withdrew into the inner desert between the Nile and the Red Sea, near the shore of which he fixed his abode on a mountain (Mount Colzim), where still stands the monastery that bears his name, Der Mar Antonios. Here, Anthony spent the last forty-five years of his life in seclusion, not so strict as Pispir, for he freely saw those who came to visit him, and he used to cross the desert to Pispir with considerable frequency. Amid the Diocletian Persecutions, 311 Anthony went to Alexandria and was conspicuous visiting those imprisoned.

Anthony was not the first ascetic or hermit. Still, he may properly be called the "Father of Monasticism" in Christianity, as he organised his disciples into a community and later, following the spread of Athanasius's hagiography, was the inspiration for similar communities throughout Egypt and elsewhere. Macius the Great was Anthony's disciple. Visitors travelled great distances to see the celebrated holy man. Anthony is said to have spoken to those of a spiritual disposition, leaving the task of addressing the more worldly visitors to Macarius. Macarius later founded a monastic community in the Scetic desert.

Anthony's fame spread and reached Emperor Constantine, who wrote to him requesting his prayers. The brethren were pleased with the Emperor's letter, but Anthony was not overawed and wrote back, encouraging the Emperor and his sons not to esteem this world but to remember the next.

When Anthony sensed his death approaching, he ordered his disciples to give his staff to Macarius of Egypt, one sheepskin cloak to Athanasius of Alexandria, and the other to Serapion of Thmuis, his disciple. According to his instructions, Anthony was interred in a grave next to his cell.

Accounts of Anthony enduring preternatural temptation during his sojourn in the Eastern Desert of Egypt inspired the often-repeated subject of the temptation of St. Anthony in Western art and literature. Anthony is said to have faced a series of unnatural temptations during his pilgrimage to the desert. The first to report on the temptation was his contemporary Athanasius of Alexandria. These events are likely full of rich metaphors or a vision or dream, in the case of the animals of the desert. Emphasis on these stories, however, began in the Middle Ages when the psychology of the individual became of greater interest. One such story was when Anthony was on a journey in the desert to find Paul of Thebes, who, according to his dream, was a better Hermit than he. Anthony had been under the impression that he was the first person to ever dwell in the desert; however, due to the dream, Anthony was called into the desert to find his "better", Paul. On his way there, he ran into two creatures in the form of a centaur and a satyr. However, chroniclers sometimes postulate that they might have been living beings. Western theology considers them to have been while travelling through the desert, Anthony first found the centaur, a "creature of mingled shape, half horse half-man", whom he asked for directions. The creature tried to speak in unintelligible language but ultimately pointed with his hand the way desired and then ran away and vanished from sight. It was interpreted as a demon trying to terrify him or a creature engendered by the desert.

Anthony found next to the satyr "a manikin with hooked snout, horned forehead, and extremities like goats's feet." This creature was peaceful and offered him fruits. When Anthony asked who he was, the satyr replied, "I'm a mortal being and one of those inhabitants of the desert whom the Gentiles, deluded by various forms of error, worship under the names of fauns, Satyrs, and Incubi. I am sent to represent my tribe. We pray you in our behalf to entreat the favour of your Lord and ours, who, we have learnt, came once to save the world, and 'whose sound has gone forth into all the earth.'" Upon hearing this, Anthony was overjoyed and rejoiced over the glory of Christ. He condemned the city of Alexandria for worshipping monsters instead of God, while beasts like the satyr spoke about Christ.

Anthony, an ascetic, lived in the tombs away from the village. There were so many demons in the cave, though, that Anthony's servant had to carry him out because they had beaten him to death. When the hermits were gathered to Anthony's corpse to mourn his death, Anthony was revived. He demanded that his servants take him back to that cave where the demons had beaten him. When he got there, he called out to the demons, and they came back as wild beasts to rip him to shreds. Suddenly, a bright light flashed, and the demons ran away. Anthony knew that the light must have come from God, and he asked God where he was before when the demons attacked him. God replied, "I was here, but I would see and abide to see thy battle, and because thou hast mainly fought and well maintained thy battle, I shall make thy name to be spread through all the world."

Anthony is credited with assisting in some miraculous healings, primarily from ergotism, a poison produced by foods like rye and wheat that can cause headaches, diarrhea, itching skin, and even gangrene. The illness became known as "St. Anthony's Fire."

Anthony walked the Camino de Santiago and is credited with establishing sixteen hospitals. Two local noblemen credited his assistance in their recovery from disease. They then founded the Hospital Brothers of St. Anthony, which specialised in nursing the victims of skin diseases in his honour.

Though Anthony did not organise or create a monastery, a community grew around him based on his example of living an ascetic and isolated life. Athanasius' biography helped propagate Anthony's ideals. Athanasius writes, "For monks, the life of Anthony is a sufficient example of asceticism- severe self-discipline and avoidance of all forms of indulgence, typically for religious reasons.

Perhaps all of my Camino pilgrimages were a search for that ascetic serenity with which only those truly on a spiritual path can resonate. I cannot attest to this in the real journeys of my pilgrimages, for I seem to have a mission that led to a different kind of outward symbolism of my inner need still hiding in the shadows of my heart's desire. I had indeed hit rock bottom physically, mentally and spiritually when the lifetime of the world value system, which I had been accustomed to all my prior lifetime, came crashing down. Be it the physical pursuits I excelled at, the education and work ethic I lived, or the Christian indoctrination engrained in my whole being, it all crumbled to nothingness in one ghastly swoop after another until I was a total wreck.

Like all illness and a loss of confidence in myself and God, I resigned myself to bandaid it all with copious amounts of alcohol, prescription drugs and toxic relationships in a desperate bid to find my way out. In time, this led to a total breakdown, and when I came out the other side, I had sworn off the drink forever.

It took some years for me to slowly recover and find a new footing in contemplation, meditation and prayers with the assistance of the programme of Alcoholics Anonymous. In time, I was well enough to return to work and have the freedom as a self-employed man again to venture on my Camino journeys, to let go of past tremors, overcome the need for prescription drugs, and search for new meaning in my life. As I had previously advised, it came as a creative outpouring in books and songs.

My pilgrimages, books, and songs have been a residual parachute to facing the reality of my spiritual condition and the need to let go of everything. Sometimes, we reach for a soft landing, fearing falling into a dark place where we may not return. Facing such fear takes courage and commitment. Finding God's path in mind for us all along is a real handover job. I now believe that the doorway to freedom and being bound to God is all in letting go. He will lead in his own good time.

Meanwhile, I shall continue to write and trust in his slow work for whatever he has in mind. I am sure I do not have to go live on a mountain in a cave like an ascetic monk to find my way or return to strive like I once did for the world's values or the applause and sense of acceptance I once craved. It is spirituality I now crave.

[Spirituality is a broad concept with room for many perspectives. It generally includes a sense of connection to something bigger than ourselves and typically involves a search for meaning in life. As such, it is a universal human experience that touches us all. People may describe a spiritual experience as *sacred* or *transcendent* or simply a deep sense of aliveness and interconnectedness.

Some may find that their spiritual life is intricately linked to their association with a church, temple, mosque, or Synagogue. Others may pray or find comfort in a personal relationship with God or a higher power. Still others seek meaning through their connections to nature or art. Like your sense of purpose, your definition of spirituality may change throughout your life, adapting to your experiences and relationships.]-AuthorLouise Delgrn, MA.MD.

Salvation has long been the quest of countless individuals throughout the ages. The lifestyle includes the withdrawal from society. To many, solitude could lead to the eventual obtainment of an ascetic goal. Solitude was not the only requirement for those intent on a spiritual life. Individuals who long for purity of heart and Christian rewards in the hereafter believed they would only yield results by keeping several other aspects of Christianity in mind. Such fundamental notions are devotion to the scriptures, both as a source of ideas and prayer recitation, as a means to tranquillity and self-control, and the value ascribed to individual freedom, love, and devotion to God.

The life of an ascetic monk like Anthony of the Desert is different from monastic life today. Ascetic Monks like Anthony were withdrawn from society for many years before people came look-ing for what they had to offer in their soul-searching. In time, those monks were drawn to teach their ways to those who wanted what they seemed to have that they did not.

When Anthony finally returned from his desert mountain retreat to visit the old hermit who had been his spiritual advisor, he was under the illusion that the older man might accompany him into the desert. The older man refused, citing his age as an excuse. It seems strange that he sought company after so long in solitary confinement. Maybe he was anxious to seek further guidance to-wards his inner calling. All we know is by what has been written of him that his only constant companion was the devil within. He had encountered a silver dish in the desert sand and left it in fear that it might be tempting to pursue the world of material possessions again. Later, he was to find some pieces of gold and leave them where he saw them, for he believed it might invite the destruction of his spiritual values. He had constant temptation like that wherever he went in the Desert. Finally, he came to an abandoned fortress by the Nile, where he took up residence. It was his last place of abode in the realm of man, though he lived there for nearly twenty years.

Anthony had changed to his ascetic state, having gone from a wealthy farm boy to a half-crazed solitary man living like an animal among the ruins of past civilisations. Those who visualised him before thought he came out of hiding once more like one with a different appearance, a new identity with his eyes on the supernatural, somewhere between human and divine. He did not come out like some old-style miracle worker. By withholding his spiritual findings, he was able to enhance his standing as an anchorite.

CHAPTER 10.

THE WAY OF SERENITY

Anthony had lived in that fortress for twenty years. Friends visited him periodically to deliver bread, but other than that, he had little human contact except for an occasional pilgrim. What went on behind that hole-in-the-wall fortress is a matter of speculation. We may draw from Athanasius's words, but ultimately, we have no answer. We now wonder how a man could survive so long with such a fanatical regime. One would think that his body would be reduced to skin and bone, his hair and beard hanging long and dirty down to his waist, eyes sunk like hollows penetrating a gaze like a madman across the desert plain. Yet when his friends came and forced him out by tearing down the fortress walls, Athanasius wrote of his appearance to the world:

[Anthony came forth from some shrine, having been led into divine mysteries and inspired by God...And when they beheld him, they were amazed to see that his body had maintained its former condition, neither fat from lack of exercise nor emaciated from fasting and combat with demons. Still, he was just as they had known him before his withdrawal. The state of his soul was one of purity, for it was not constricted by grief, relaxed by pleasure, or affected by either laughter or sadness. Anthony maintained utter equilibrium like one guided by reason and steadfast as that accorded with nature.]

There was a man who was hardened physically to the way of the desert but fashioned internally by ascetic practice; a man with a certain freshness and spiritual perfection was already evident. The image of a raving madman had been put to rest. Anthony had transformed himself into a living picture of Christ.

Anthony had, by example, persuaded many to take up the mantle of an anchorite and follow in his footsteps. Athanasius wrote: "The desert was made into a city by monks, who left their people and registered themselves for citizenship in the heavens." A new society was thus born, one who owed no allegiance to no man save he who was prepared to dedicate himself to cultivating the blue flower of ascites, that symbol of calmness, serenity and purity.

Those men and women bent towards contemplation, meditation, and religiosity have been inspired to seek lives of solitude since ancient times, moved by the belief that spiritual fulfilment can be found in rejecting society's expectations and encumbrances. The desert fathers and mothers, the earliest known Christian solitaries, were inspirational role models for the professional contemplatives of the Middle Ages. They withdrew from the world for the same fundamental reason as their medieval counterparts did: that they might better come to know themselves and, through that self-knowledge, generate a more intimate connection with God.

Anchorites were men and women who sought to withdraw from the world as much as was practicable, often (although not always) to a small, four-walled cell adjoining a religious building. Sometimes referred to as the medieval world's living dead, many spiritual thinkers have written for and about them, inspired partly by the theatrical notion of grave-like spatial fixity upon which the vocation is founded.

In contrast to the eremitic seclusion of hermits, who could theoretically move locations, anchorites were permanently enclosed within the walls of their cell or 'anchor-hold'. They remained in the world yet were manifestly not of it. They retreated to a spatially restricted spiritual arena to confront the very worst in them. They engaged in this spiritual struggle for themselves and the wider world, which, paradoxically, the vocation was developed to reject.

Our knowledge about anchorites is based on two broad kinds of evidence: archaeological and documentary. Neither type of evidence affords us the objective 'truth' about how anchorites lived but instead offers us a series of ideological pictures or subjective 'truths' about the vocation.

Some of these pictures do indeed construct the medieval anchor-hold as a solitary death cell, in which the hermit endures simply as a living corpse locked up in death-like darkness. Yet others reveal the less critically prominent but equally valid depiction of a busy man or woman who willingly interrupts devotions to be of spiritual service to a steady stream of visitors. As the vocation was never standardised and never constituted a religious order (although members of religious orders could and did become recluses), it would be unwise to make wide-sweeping generalisations about anchorites in their individual cells, documents, or lives. Nevertheless, much of the surviving evidence presents anchoritism as highly esteemed by the surrounding community, a community which, after all, enabled the vocation to exist and persist in both economic and practical terms.

The earliest prehistoric person, or caveman as they come to be known, indulged in an anchorite practice, depicted as drawings on cave walls since the earliest recorded history of man. The cave drawings in France date back 32,000 years, are in Grotte Chauvet- Pont d'Arc, located in a limestone plateau of the meandering Ardèche River in southern France, and extend to an area of approximately 8500 square meters. While the artwork in the caves in Marlos, Indonesia, was until recently proven to be the oldest, being more than 40,000 old, these have been superseded by cave drawings and artifacts found in Kakadu National Park that have been carbon-dated to prove they are more than 70,000 years old.

So, early cave dwellers who were proven to live and painted their dreams and aspirations on cave walls between 17,000 and 70,000 years ago have something in common with the earliest recorded anchorites, like the third-century AD Saint Anthony the Anchorite (251–356), also known as "Anthony of the Desert," and who has the reputation of Christianity's "Father of Monasticism." Hilarion (Gaza, 291—Cyprus, 371) is known as the founder of anchoritic life in Palestine.

From what we know of ancient man, they retreated to cave dwellings and drew their thoughts and aspirations on the concave wall. These drawings depict animals, hunting parties, symbols and signs of links with nature, the sky, images of God and their self-image and likeness. Much of their drawings were completed in the dark, with maybe only a flickering fire light or inner spirit guiding creation. Whilst what is written about this is our speculation, what has been carried down the ages is their link with the land and the natural environment.

Perhaps it is not such a far stretch of the imagination to accept that they, too, were anchorites in search of spiritual fulfilment and learning to come to terms with their natural world while living in cave-like cells, as did Anthony of the Desert and the Desert Fathers. Escaping far from the madding crowd had always been a habit of those bent on a spiritual quest to fulfil creative pursuits.

Whilst many of the world's population today live in small apartments, unit dwellings or bedsitters, it is more challenging to live like an anchorite of old due to the many distractions of modern living. In the home, we are endlessly distracted by night lights, television, radio and mobile phones, and the never-ending bombardment of materialism to distract us from our inward journey. We habitually indulge in food beyond our needs, lack sufficient sleep, drink copious quantities of coffee, drink too much alcohol or smoke cigarettes on the pretext that we need these distractions as comfort to relieve our stress-filled lifestyle.

It is not difficult to be caught up in the rat race, having to meet work deadlines, pay an ever-increasing pile of bills and being locked into financing an unnecessary need for a bigger home, more excellent car, boat or lengthy resort holiday, from halfway around the world to find peace. What if we switched off the light, turned off the TV, radio, computer, or mobile phone and retreated into a dark space to draw images that appear on the wall from the skylight through our windows, or maybe sit gazing out on the movement of a tree or listen to the sounds of the night. I wonder if we could become just for a few moments and anchorite without going anywhere but remain like the caveman of old in our cell cave like the Desert Fathers.

Of course, any man or woman is at perfect liberty to live as they please. I am not spiritually qualified to tell anyone how they should live; however, many of us might have been much more balanced and spiritually sound if we had followed the pathway of an anchorite. Though more adventurous or nomadic, I suspect that my journey had taken on qualities of living as a pilgrim and absorbed some of the anchorites ' peculiarities, which has set me apart from my fellowman for a time.   The way of the anchorite and their hidden habits in closed cells or caves is perhaps best summed up in an eighteenth-century Chinese novel: 'The Dream of the Red Chamber:'

"He had been dreaming and then woke up. He found himself in the interior of a temple. On one side, a beggar dressed in the robes of a Taoist monk stood out. He was lame and was killing fleas. The dreamer asked him who he was and what place they were in. The monk answered: " I don't know who I am, nor where we are. I only know that the road is long." The dreamer understood. He cut off his hair with his sword and followed the strange.

Life experience has taught me that I must still determine who I am and where I am going. And yet, I am surrounded by the journey, for it has become my sole reality, erasing all memory of where I might belong today in everyday ordinary life. Sometimes, I find myself entering another space of the lame beggar killing fleas. Here, I can practice what can be described as ' a game of words,' for I retire to do this amid my engagement with my earthly senses. It is a game I play to retain the reality of my fantasies. It is the language of which I can give the language of inner value some new meaning to keep me grounded from the surroundings of distractions. It is in those moments that I am the captain of my fate. The maker of my destiny, it is then I am alive like an anchorite; I am not alone and in need of no other.

I remember, whilst walking my first Camino in 2013, meeting up with a man who had walked the 800km way to Santiago de Compostela nine times. He was tall and handsome with the appearance of purity or more like a statue of Michelangelo's David than a saint. He carried no knapsack, just one spare robe, as monks do. He had no money or food and relied on the charity of others to donate to see him through. Everywhere I went, he seemed to be there before me. Brother John, he called himself, was a follower of Mother Teresa of Calcutta. He had a daily routine of commencing his travels in meditative walking before the dawning light, arriving at his preplanned destination in the later afternoon. Before approaching cafes and restaurant owners en route to supply him with a meal or seeking a place to sleep, he always headed for a small church to mediate and pray to Jesus in solitude, asking for guidance.

Brother John always looked spick and span with his robe clean and well-pressed. I asked him how he managed to do that, and he said there is always someone in any village or city who willingly washes his clothing and irons it, expecting nothing in return. He did many charitable things to compensate for his dependence on donations by helping those less fortunate. John was, by profession, a university lecturer who returned to the occupation in his native Hungary from time to time to teach before heading off somewhere in the world where people needed help. He had even travelled to Australia and worked in our red-light district. When he found out I was an Australian, he just remarked. "Kings Cross is a bad place."

Brother John had no concept of time, for he didn't have a watch or mobile phone and depended on Mother Nature to guide him. My last contact with him was in Borgos, Spain. He had given me a religious card with the Sacred Heart of Jesus on one side and a prayer in Hungarian on the other. As he handed it to me, he said, " Jesus loves you, Doug." And then he just vanished, and I never saw him on my Camino journey again.

I am chastened by the words of Carl Yung in his 'Alchemical Studies: "A Chinese can always fall back on the authority of the whole civilisation. If he starts the long way, he is doing what is recognised as the best thing he could be. But if he is earnest about it, the Westerner who wishes to set out this way has all the authority against him- intellectually and morally. And religious…

The individual must devote himself to the way with all his energy, for it is only by using his integrity that he can go further, and his integrity alone can guarantee that his way will not be an absurd misadventure."

So, it is to break away from the shell of one's existence by doing something new. Our ego ideas can't do well for us, nor do our feelings of worth and values. We often hesitate to venture beyond the limits of our self-restrictions. Of course, there are abstract limits to what we can do, but the fact that we do not have wings to fly does not mean we cannot use our imagination in ways to fly like a bird on the wing. Growth in our character and the consequent deep satisfaction depends on discovering and facing our masked fear.

So it is that I tell myself "I must" may sometimes be the wholesome urge for great creativity. In all sound efforts to do something new, I must remember the principles of taking small steps. In looking ahead to new experiences, I begin to widen my view of the world, bringing me beyond my former limitations. Now, it is not to think of some quick and easy journey to the new realms, for that is the selfish wish for quick triumph. It tends to defeat my ends, especially when my reaction is " I cannot." It is my experience to reach for goals even little by little. It is never a smooth path, but if I trust being led by a power greater than myself, I can attain greatness for my soul self, and my creative output is then to guide better those needing my services.

Another realisation is that I've come to believe in accepting the reason for my creative outpouring. The calamity of my life experience led to collapse and catapulted me on adventurers to help heal my wounded self. For a time, I felt that I would soon die, and I confess that for a time, I desired the end to ease my troubled mind. In my cry for help, the answer came through journaling my feelings, ultimately leading to writing books of varying genres, and this process is still in play. I was keen to publish and wanted to get as many books in the marketplace as quickly as possible. Instead of baby steps, I tried long, quick leaps to get the written word out there. I bypassed editing and proofreading due to my fear of death, for I was determined to leave behind more than just a headstone. Of course, the ethos was linked to holding on to ego notions.

Once I recovered and found the belief in a spiritual path, I discovered the ways of inner peace, and my output of books and songs increased fourfold. So, I sought professional help in editing and proofreading, which is more conducive to appearing to the reader than my former approach. I soon lost the fear and need to seek applause for my writing. In the first decade of writing books, marketing and promotion, I sold many books, but since COVID-19, the sales have slowed. The lack of sales doesn't faze me anymore. I am a writer for a creative outlet for those who need help and some guidance from my life experience, particularly when it comes to alcoholism, pain and suffering. I don't need the applause, for when I reviewed my former life, I realised it all led to emptiness. It does not matter now if I am first or last, winning or losing, making money or not; it's all about progress towards spirituality. It could be what the cave dwellers found in drawing their imaginative figures on concave walls, and it could be all the Anchorites sought in their dark being instead of doing at all.

Perhaps we have had the wrong perspective in our constant striving for material answers to life. We may gaze at a flock of seagulls soaring over the ocean waves and, in our absent-mindedness, vaguely watch them as "just gulls," but if we watch first one and then another, something will seem to open up. Then, we may become familiar with the pattern and rhythm of their flight.

Our education system has us believe we must try to overcome difficulties. If we played tennis, we felt we had to try. The result was a stiff body, an entire effort, and a jerky swing at the ball until someone said,' Play with a loose arm.'All at once, the ball went skimming across the net to the far court, not once but repeatedly, and I found myself in the zone of ease and grace. Surprisingly, my arm seemed to be working independently without my meddling. It seemed to know what to do, to judge strength and direction without my help.

Sometimes, answers come to us without end. Why do I not take more time to contemplate and even think about doing something before I attempt it? Indeed, the key to my private reality might lie in an apparent simple skill: letting the senses remain unfettered by purpose. I would like to know whether my eyes and ears have their wisdom.

The soul of man must hasten to creation.
Out of the formless stone, when the artist united
himself with stone,
Spring is always a new form of life. From the soul of
Man that is joined to the soul of stone;
Out of the meaningless practical shapes of all that
Is living or lifeless
Joined with the artist's eye, new life, new form,
New colour.
Out of the sea of sound, the life of music,
Out of the slimy mud of words, out of the sleet
And hail of verbal imprecision,
Approximate thoughts and feelings, words that
Have taken the place of thoughts and feelings,
There spring the perfect order of speech and the
Luxury of incarnation.

Lord, shall we not bring these gifts to Your service?
Shall we not bring to Your service our powers
For life, for dignity, grace and order,
And intellectual pleasures at the senses?
The Lord who created must wish us to create
Which is already His service in creating
To employ our His service in creating.
For man is joined in spirit and body.
Therefore, it must serve as spirit and body.
Visible and invisible, two worlds His temple;
You must not deny the body.

Now you shall see the Temple completed
After much striving, after many obstacles,
For the work of creation is never without travail;
The formed stone, the visible crucifix,
The dressed altar, the lifting light;

Light Light

The visible reminder of Invisible Light.

T. S. Eliot, 18881965. English Poet
Choruses from " The Rock."

About the Author.

Doug McPhillips, poet, singer, songwriter, and author, began his journey of discovery over a decade ago after having had life-changing experiences.

The many tracks he has traversed through the Northern Hemisphere and down under in Australia and New Zealand have resulted in the facts and fiction of this novel.

Doug has recorded and sung songs interrelated to his many works, with majestic melodies in an authentic Australian style.

Doug has written several novels, two books of poems, a travel guide and three albums of his songs, all inspired by his adventurers.

Doug is an adventurer who divides his time between family and friends, his creative pursuits, and those who benefit most from his efforts and experience.

Reference material for this book includes:

Alcoholics Anonymous, 4th Edition AA World Service, 1976

As Bill sees it. 18th Print, AA World Service. 2017.

Daily Reflections, 11th print, AA World Service. 2014.

Journey to the Inner Mountain, Hodder & Staughton, James Cowan, 2002.

The Choice is Always Ours, Jove Publications.1997

Santiago Traveller: Ingram Sparke, Doug McPhillips. 2018

References of Authors within the content of this book.

Google Research from Authors unknown.